mornings with God:
daily Bible devotional for men

# mornings with God: daily Bible devotional for men

## 365 Devotions to Inspire Your Day

**JONATHAN PUDDLE**

ROCKRIDGE PRESS

**FOR MY SONS, JAMES
AND RUUBEN.**
May you always find Jesus in the
pages of scripture, and may
you find in Jesus a better way to be
a man. I am so proud of you both.

# Introduction

**I haven't always enjoyed** reading the Bible. In fact, I gave up on it for years.

I grew up in a Christian home and I knew God loved me, but in my late teens and early twenties, the faith of my childhood didn't seem robust enough for the realities of my grown-up life. I had been taught that God's Word would answer all my questions, but it didn't. I loved God, but the more I read the Bible, the more God seemed angry and distant—while rigidly enforcing arbitrary rules—which left me confused and frustrated. I put the Bible down and told God he would have to teach me how to find love in it again.

Some years later, I experienced a renewal in my faith. Jesus captured my attention and my affection in a new way, and I was drawn back to the Bible. When I opened it, I found a totally different book! To my surprise, grace, love, and hope spilled out of every page. I also saw a new way to be a man.

How's that "man" thing working out for *you* these days?

It seems to be a confusing time for men. Growing up in the eighties, my role models were cool, strong, and unemotional, like Sly Stallone. Today, we're expected to be tender and compassionate, like Paul Rudd. That's not an easy pivot for anyone, and we have precious few good role models. In Jesus, I have discovered an inspiring blend of passion and peace, strength and gentleness, wisdom and wit. He is the kind of man I want to be.

My goal in this devotional is to point you to Jesus through scripture. Although the Bible is full of timeless proverbs and useful instructions, I think they function best as a reflection of God's character, not as rules for us to follow. To that end, each day I will give you something that I hope draws you into fellowship with Jesus and helps you locate him within the pages of this ancient holy text. Whether you're picking the Bible up for the first time (or the first time in a while) or you're a seasoned Bible reader, I hope you will meet God afresh and find encouragement and hope each day.

## How to Use This Book

This book was designed as a morning devotional: a quick moment (two minutes, really) to pause and connect with God before you get into the busyness of the day. You can use it anytime you like, of course, and even come back to the same reading again more than once in the day. It's totally up to you. Readings follow a loosely thematic order.

Start by turning to the day's devotional and read the title.

Take a deep breath in, then breathe out. Try to let go of any tension you may be holding.

Read the passage of scripture and the reflection that accompanies it.

Take another deep breath in and release it.

Read the passage of scripture once more. Then pause and spend a few seconds in silence, allowing the words to linger in your mind and settle into your heart. God might even speak to you.

Most days, this will take a maximum of two minutes. Peppered throughout the book are a number of slightly longer reflections. They're topics that I wanted to dwell on a little more, and they include a section called "Live Out the Word," which includes some questions to ponder.

I'm glad you're here. Let's get into it!

# 1 | God Is Only Good

> *This is the message we have heard from him and declare to you: God is light; in him there is no darkness at all.*
>
> **— 1 JOHN 1:5**

I don't know what kind of life you've had—a charmed one, a painful one, or somewhere in between—but whatever it is, your life has shaped your understanding of God. Each one of your days tells a story of what God (and other people) is like. Is he kind? Is he safe? Am I safe? Today, see if you can hit pause on your preconceived notions of God and life, and simply lean into hope and light, however they are available to you today.

# 2 | It Starts in a Playground

> *In the beginning God created the heavens and the earth.*
>
> **— GENESIS 1:1**

This planet, full of beauty and wonder, brimming with exquisite pleasures and delights, is God's gift to us. It pleased God for you and me to take up space in a world meant for our enjoyment and exploration. Before you worked to earn anything, God offered you life on this good earth for free. As you go about your day, consider that everything you see, touch, taste, smell, or hear exists because it was God's idea in the first place, and he simply gave it to you.

# 3 | Love Starts the Process

*We love because he first loved us.*

**— 1 JOHN 4:19**

As a young man, I didn't want to disappoint God, so I tried very hard to be good. As I grew in the knowledge and experience of God's love, the pressure to perform began to relax while, oddly, my life became more righteous. Basking in the love of God caused love to flow out of me, and love—it turns out—is the heart of righteousness. Our lives and our hopes start with God's love. We're only ever responding to what he's already done for us. Have you felt this love? Would you like to? You can ask him for more.

# 4 | Guideposts for Love

*All Scripture is God-breathed and is useful for teaching, rebuking, correcting, and training in righteousness, so that the servant of God may be thoroughly equipped for every good work.*

**— 2 TIMOTHY 3:16–17**

To identify God's love and grow in righteousness, we need tools and training. We need guideposts. The stories, poems, parables, and characters of the Bible are relatable and timeless. If we read honestly and carefully, we can find Jesus—and our ourselves—in the pages of scripture, along with an invitation to lean into God's love and let it transform us. Through the study of scripture, your daily life can be filled and informed by the breath of God.

## 5 | God and His Word

> *In the beginning was the Word, and the Word was with God, and the Word was God.*
>
> **— JOHN 1:1**

Before interviewing people on my podcast, I read their books or watch their YouTube videos. People's words help reveal what they are like and give me insight into their interests and passions. God's Word is the same; it reveals him to us. When God created the world, he spoke it into being. His Word made everything he had dreamed of become real. Every time we read or hear the Word of God, we learn more about what God is really like. But his Word is not a book; it's a person.

## 6 | A Word That Walks

> *The Word became flesh and made his dwelling among us. We have seen his glory, the glory of the one and only Son, who came from the Father, full of grace and truth.*
>
> **— JOHN 1:14**

I grew up in church in the eighties with Psalty the Singing Songbook. Picture a giant blue book with arms and legs and a face on the spine. It was silly. Funny thing is, like Psalty, God's Word also walks and talks because God's Word is a person, a human being, like you and me. The Word that created all things reveals God and is full of grace and truth. He came and lived among us. He is Jesus Christ, God-made-flesh.

# 7 | Focusing on Jesus

> *You study the Scriptures diligently because you think that in them you have eternal life. These are the very Scriptures that testify about me.*
>
> **— JOHN 5:39**

As we explore the Bible over the next year, we're going to find all kinds of practical and encouraging words of wisdom, worship, and insight. The Bible is a wonderful holy text, but its full effectiveness is not found simply in the wisdom it offers. Its true power lies in its witness to Jesus Christ, the living Word of God. He still speaks to us today, and the Bible trains us to hear and identify his voice, amid all the others. What is Jesus saying to you today?

# 8 | Hide-and-Seek

> *You will seek me and find me when you seek me with all your heart.*
>
> **— JEREMIAH 29:13**

When my children were young, we played a lot of hide-and-seek. Most kids don't hide very well, and they giggle the whole time. I suspect they want to be found—they enjoy the chase because they anticipate the excitement of our company. I believe God is the same. He wants to be found, and he has promised that we will find him. And by the way, seeking with all our hearts is not a condition that God puts on us; it's just an assessment of what the process will require.

# 9 | Bringing Our Needs to God

> *In the morning, LORD, you hear my voice; in the morning
> I lay my requests before you and wait expectantly.*
>
> **— PSALM 5:3**

As we seek God and learn more about him, we discover an invitation to come to him with our needs and requests. He welcomes men like us, needy and imperfect. Of course, our prayers aren't always answered in the ways we might want, but it is a comfort to know that God hears and treasures our prayers. We are even invited to be expectant. Do you expect God to do good things in your life? If not, why might that be?

# 10 | Strong Arms

> *The eternal God is your refuge, and underneath
> are the everlasting arms.*
>
> **— DEUTERONOMY 33:27**

The men who were in our lives when we were growing up shaped many of our expectations about God. If they were kind and caring, you'll probably find it easier to see God that way. If they were cold and distant, or angry and abusive, there's a good chance that you'll expect the same of God. There's no shame in that; it's just how your brain makes sense of the world. But God is a safe refuge. He holds us and supports us through all of life's hardships. Even if we don't see him there, he is strong and good and present.

# 11 | A Free Gift

> *All are justified freely by his grace through the redemption that came by Christ Jesus.*
>
> **— ROMANS 3:24**

Scripture talks a lot about grace and for good reason. God's graceful nature freely forgives sin, and his gift of grace helps us overcome it every day, filling our lives with love, freedom, and power. But unlike almost everything else in our lives, it's not something you must earn or repay. Grace is not the Corvette you buy in your sixties after you've worked a lifetime; it's more like the remote-controlled toy car your parents gave you for Christmas–just because they loved you. If grace is difficult to comprehend, it might be because you're more accustomed to working hard and earning things than you are to freely receiving them. Grace is a free gift that God has given to everyone because he wanted to. It might have cost him a lot to give it, but that was his choice. Our choice is simply to receive with open hands.

## Live Out the Word

Do you spend more time trying to earn God's grace or enjoying God's grace?

Make a list of gifts you have received. Which one is the most important to you? Why?

Find someone in your life who is in need. Give them something meaningful, with no strings attached. How did this make you feel? What does that tell you about God?

# 12 | Owning What We've Done

> *Then David said to Nathan, "I have sinned against the LORD." Nathan replied, "The LORD has taken away your sin. You are not going to die."*
>
> **— 2 SAMUEL 12:13**

God's grace frees us from sin, and his radical forgiveness means that nothing is ever held against us. This is incredible news, and it should move us toward honest accountability. If we are not sincere about what we've done—the hurt we've caused others, how we have fallen short of the standard of love—then how can we really appropriate this grace? God invites us to admit our mistakes, walk in his light, and breathe freely.

# 13 | The Standard of Love

> *This is how we know what love is: Jesus Christ laid down his life for us. And we ought to lay down our lives for our brothers and sisters.*
>
> **— 1 JOHN 3:16**

I love whiskey, cigars, and science fiction. I love my wife and my kids. I also love God. Clearly, there's a range of loves. I don't love cigars the same way I love my wife. It helps to have a clear definition, a standard. John offers one by pointing to Jesus: To love means to lay down your life for others, to die (whether literally or figuratively) so that others might live. Scary and impossible? Maybe. But also . . . challenge accepted!

## 14 | In a League of His Own

*Who among the gods is like you, L*ORD*?*
*Who is like you—majestic in holiness, awesome*
*in glory, working wonders?*

**— EXODUS 15:11**

There's a lot of pressure placed on men. Be strong, be cool, provide for your people, care for others without appearing weak—the list goes on. I take great relief in knowing that God hasn't put these pressures on me. He invites me to be me and to let him be him. He's the one worthy of my worship and my praise. No athlete, movie star, politician, or business mogul even comes close. And they don't have to.

## 15 | The Pinnacle of Creation

*Then God said, "Let us make mankind in our image,*
*in our likeness, so that they may rule over*
*the fish in the sea and the birds in the sky, over*
*the livestock and all the wild animals, and*
*over all the creatures that move along the ground."*

**— GENESIS 1:26**

Once God had created all the framework and details of his beautiful world, he capped it off with his most remarkable creation yet: humanity. We were made to be like God himself, full of power, majesty, freedom, and love. Your birthright, as a human being made in God's image, is to graciously rule over the earth and everything in it.

## 16 | Everything We Need

*His divine power has given us everything we need*
*for a godly life through our knowledge*
*of him who called us by his own glory and goodness.*

**— 2 PETER 1:3**

Sometimes I think Peter got this one wrong. I do not always feel like I have everything I need for a godly life. But I have learned that although my feelings should always be listened to, they should not always be believed or acted upon. God has called us his own and given us unlimited access to himself, which is where we find everything we could ever need for every kind of challenge we face.

## 17 | Mountain Climbing

*The Sovereign LORD is my strength; he makes my feet like*
*the feet of a deer, he enables me to tread on the heights.*

**— HABAKKUK 3:19**

For many years, I wanted to climb Mount Everest. I thought it would be an incredible challenge to overcome. Then I got married, had kids, and learned the facts about Everest (the costs, the survival ratio, etc.). I decided I have enough challenges in front of me, which, incidentally, probably won't kill me. For the challenges of today, God is our strength. He steadies our feet and helps us overcome every obstacle, great and small.

# 18 | A Good and Gentle Teacher

> *I will instruct you and teach you in the way you should go; I will counsel you with my loving eye on you.*
>
> **— PSALM 32:8**

I've had some teachers who weren't very kind. I had one who was downright abusive, and I had to work through it in therapy years later. Thankfully, God is not a toxic teacher; he is kind and constantly affirming. His instruction, guidance, and counsel are full of grace and love. If his teaching ever chafes, it's probably because we're on a bad path. Have you experienced God guiding you peacefully? I hope so.

# 19 | Governed by Love

> *For the Spirit God gave us does not make us timid, but gives us power, love and self-discipline.*
>
> **— 2 TIMOTHY 1:7**

As if making us in his own image—to be like him—wasn't enough, God has given us his own Spirit to make him real within us. If you find yourself fearful and timid about living life, afraid of stumbling or making a mistake, that's understandable. Fear is a natural thing; there's no shame in it. But the Holy Spirit invites us—and enables us—to live beyond the limits of fear in supernatural courage, power, and self-discipline, all governed by love.

## 20 | Mindful Intentionality

> *Now this is what the Lord Almighty says:*
> *"Give careful thought to your ways."*
>
> **— HAGGAI 1:5**

God made us powerful and free, intended for us to rule over creation, and provides fresh grace for each day. That sounds like a pretty good deal to me. Still, the Holy Spirit calls us to be mindful and intentional, to give thought to our ways. God has designed us with a conscience and given us self-control. It's our responsibility to use these incredible gifts wisely, to not become drunk on power or privilege but to pay attention to our ways and observe the impact of our actions.

## 21 | Created Good, Still Good

> *God saw all that he had made, and it*
> *was very good. And there was evening, and*
> *there was morning—the sixth day.*
>
> **— GENESIS 1:31**

There's a belief held by some folks that all humanity became bad and wretched because of Adam and Eve's original sin and that creation itself is now cursed. I think that gives far too much credit to evil. God called his creation "good," so what can stand against that? Are we wounded and in need of healing? Sure. Lost and in need of a savior? Absolutely. But nothing in creation is bad or cursed. God calls us very good. Remember that.

## 22 | Loving Justice

> *The LORD loves righteousness and justice;*
> *the earth is full of his unfailing love.*
>
> **— PSALM 33:5**

God cares deeply about the harm that is done to his children. Whether the evils of racism, corporate greed, government corruption, exploitation of workers, or human trafficking, God desires righteousness and justice for all. As he fills us with his love, it should move us to care about the things he cares about. We have all experienced injustice to some degree, and we have all committed acts of evil against others. God's love invites each of us to become agents of justice and righteousness on earth, right now, today.

## 23 | Asking for Wisdom

> *If any of you lacks wisdom, you should ask God,*
> *who gives generously to all without*
> *finding fault, and it will be given to you.*
>
> **— JAMES 1:5**

As a child, I thought adults had it all figured out. As a father and husband, I know the truth: We're flying by the seat of our pants much of the time. From difficult situations at work to challenges with our spouses and kids, life presents countless obstacles we must overcome or work around. God offers his boundless wisdom to all who ask for it and doesn't shame us for needing his help.

# 24 | All Work Is Sacred Worship

> *The LORD God took the man and put him in the Garden of Eden to work it and take care of it.*
>
> **— GENESIS 2:15**

Do you love your job? I've been employed in a range of professions, and some were more life-giving than others. The first job that the first man had was to tend the garden God had created. What an incredible privilege! God invites us to see all the work of our hands as sacred. I hope you find moments of meaningful contribution and connection in your work today. Whatever your profession or employment status, your faithfulness is worship to the Lord.

# 25 | Relentless Hope

> *Let us hold unswervingly to the hope we profess, for he who promised is faithful.*
>
> **— HEBREWS 10:23**

Life can be hard. Financial problems, physical illness, and difficult relationships are just a few of the things that threaten us each day. Finding hope in the face of over-whelming circumstances feels impossible some days. Yet we are reminded to hold tight to our hope in Jesus, the one who promised to be with us always. Developing relentless hope is brave, courageous work, and the world needs more men filled with hope in the goodness and faithfulness of God. How robust is your hope? What could make it stronger?

## 26 | Good News for All

> But the angel said to them, "Do not be afraid. I bring you good news that will cause great joy for all the people."
>
> **— LUKE 2:10**

Practically every time an angel turns up in the Bible, the angel starts by saying, "Do not be afraid!" Clearly, God understands that an encounter with divinity terrifies and overwhelms us. Is it our shame that causes this response, or the unworthiness we feel standing in the presence of pure love? Whatever the cause, God meets us at our level, lifts our eyes to look into his, and invites us to move past fear into trust and hope. God is here, and that's good news.

## 27 | Salvation for All

> For the grace of God has appeared that offers salvation to all people.
>
> **— TITUS 2:11**

God has always offered his grace freely to all people, but humanity's fear and unworthiness held us back. To convince us once and for all of his good intentions toward us, God took on our frail human form in his Son, Jesus. Also known as Emmanuel, or "God with us," Jesus shows us that God's gift of grace is available here and now for everyone who wants it. What has the grace of God made possible in your life? What would your life be like without Jesus?

# 28 | Not What We Deserve

*Some became fools through their rebellious ways
and suffered affliction because of their iniquities....
Then they cried to the LORD in their trouble, and
he saved them from their distress. He sent out his word
and healed them; he rescued them from the grave.*

**— PSALM 107:17, 19–20**

I don't know about you, but over the years I have fallen into some pretty deep holes. Some of them I even dug for myself. When I admitted my mistakes, humbled myself, and turned to God, he rescued me and redeemed me from my stupidity. I'm very thankful that we don't get what we deserve; I much prefer grace.

# 29 | Growing Up

*And Jesus grew in wisdom and stature,
and in favor with God and man.*

**— LUKE 2:52**

If you look back on yourself as a child or teenager, how do you feel about that boy? Are you embarrassed by things you did as a youth, or do you have compassion for that young man moving slowly toward maturity? The simple truth is that all of us must grow up. Even Jesus, God in human flesh, was a young boy once and had to develop as we do. In time, he found his place in his community. Growing up means trying new things and sometimes making mistakes.

## 30 | A Path of Peace

*The LORD makes firm the steps of the
one who delights in him.*

**— PSALM 37:23**

I once crossed a frozen lake a bit too late in the season.
When I realized my mistake, I turned to go back, only to
see the city lights illuminating my footsteps, each now full
of surface meltwater. Returning on that path was way too
scary of an option. I had little choice but to push on and
trust God to keep me safe. My life has often felt that way.
The good news is that God has promised that all those who
enjoy him will find their path marked by peace, confidence,
hope, and security.

## 31 | When It All Falls Apart

*When I heard these things, I sat down and wept.
For some days I mourned and
fasted and prayed before the God of heaven.*

**— NEHEMIAH 1:4**

Sometimes it all just goes wrong. Tragic circumstances can
make us feel utterly defeated. When the bad news is simply
too much to bear, it is good and right to mourn and lament.
A heart that is healthy will feel grief and sadness over terrible things. Oftentimes, as men, it seems we have not been
given permission to cry when we hurt. I give you permission
today to respond wholeheartedly to tragic news. God cries
with you.

## 32 | When We've Made It Worse

*Pardon your servant, Lord. What can I say, now that Israel has been routed by its enemies?*

**— JOSHUA 7:8**

Sometimes when it all goes wrong, we know that we contributed to it. Whether it was entirely our fault or not, our efforts don't always help. Joshua, one of the leaders of Israel, was no stranger to this. He demonstrated a wise path forward, acknowledging his hopelessness and asking God to pardon him. The truth, of course, is not that God holds anything against us but that our prideful self-absorption sows destruction in our lives. God invites us to turn from this.

## 33 | The Wisest Approach

*But the wisdom that comes from heaven is first of all pure; then peace-loving, considerate, submissive, full of mercy and good fruit, impartial and sincere.*

**— JAMES 3:17**

When we seek God for guidance, he doesn't withhold it. By waiting on the Holy Spirit, we can find strategies and tactics that will cut past favoritism and bring peace and goodness to all involved. If you are facing a tough challenge and none of the solutions presented seem like good fruit, rest assured that the Spirit has not yet brought clarity. Keep seeking God's wisdom, and in good time a path forward will be made clear.

# 34 | A Cleansing Shower

> *Cleanse me with hyssop, and I will be clean;*
> *wash me, and I will be whiter than snow.*
>
> **— PSALM 51:7**

On bad days, walking through this world can feel like trudging through a sewer. Two common temptations, power and pornography, can leave us feeling especially slimy when we trip up. But God doesn't hold our failures against us. His love washes us clean and restores our dignity and worth. If you're feeling dirty—whether from your own actions or someone else's—ask Jesus to cleanse your mind, body, soul, and spirit. He will wash you and restore you to your original glory.

# 35 | A Tattoo of Remembrance

> *Can a mother forget the baby at her breast and have*
> *no compassion on the child she has borne?*
> *Though she may forget, I will not forget you! See, I*
> *have engraved you on the palms of my hands.*
>
> **— ISAIAH 49:15–16A**

Did you know God has your name tattooed on his hands? That's pretty badass. Not only is the palm a very painful place to get a tattoo, but God also declares that he loves us even more than a mother loves her own baby. When you feel alone, rejected, cut off, or forgotten, remember that God will never forget or abandon you.

## 36 | Do Not Judge

*You, therefore, have no excuse, you who pass judgment on someone else, for at whatever point you judge another, you are condemning yourself, because you who pass judgment do the same things.*

**— ROMANS 2:1**

Do you believe that people are generally doing the best they can? I never used to. I thought, "If everyone was working as hard as me to be kind and righteous, the world would be a better place!" Then someone accused me of not caring, and it broke my heart because I knew I was doing everything I could. This changed my perspective. We're all just trying our best out here, so don't judge anyone.

## 37 | Honest and True

*God is not a human, that he should lie, not a human being, that he should change his mind. Does he speak and then not act? Does he promise and not fulfill?*

**— NUMBERS 23:19**

It is acceptable in parts of our culture to overpromise and underdeliver, to mislead others for the sake of the deal. Whether the dishonest mechanic or the sly accountant, God understands our temptation to self-protecting deceit but calls us to a higher standard of integrity. Honesty, responsibility, and follow-through are very important to God because he is that way himself—consistent, genuine, and trustworthy in all his ways.

# 38 | The "Man" for the Job

> For if you remain silent at this time, relief
> and deliverance for the Jews will arise from another
> place, but you and your father's family will
> perish. And who knows but that you have come to
> your royal position for such a time as this?
>
> **— ESTHER 4:14**

Esther was chosen to join the harem of the king of Persia, and she used the opportunity to inform him of systemic and intentional injustices that were killing her people. It's a dramatic story, and we're invited into it. What evils do you have a vantage point on? What do you see that needs to change? Perhaps you can speak up.

# 39 | Run Away!

> Flee from sexual immorality. All other sins a
> person commits are outside the body, but whoever
> sins sexually, sins against their own body.
>
> **— 1 CORINTHIANS 6:18**

God created our bodies with the ability and desire to have sex. The orgasm was his idea! The pleasures we can enjoy are meant to reflect something of the divine ecstasy of oneness with God. Our bodies long for it and it is good, but life offers us cheap and quick imitations that don't require vulnerability or intimacy. They leave us feeling defiled and unworthy of the very love we crave. Run from these temptations and pursue purer pleasures.

## 40 | Have You Seen God?

> *No one has ever seen God, but the one and only*
> *Son, who is himself God and is in closest relationship*
> *with the Father, has made him known.*
>
> **— JOHN 1:18**

According to the Hebrew scriptures (our Old Testament), Adam and Eve, Noah, Abraham and Sarah, Hagar, Moses, and more all saw God face-to-face. Either John had a bad memory or else he was trying to communicate, "If you haven't seen Jesus, you ain't seen nothing." Take all your expectations of what God is like, how he works, and what he'll do, and lay them at the feet of Jesus. He will show us the truth.

## 41 | Salvation Is Here!

> *For God did not send his Son into the world to condemn*
> *the world, but to save the world through him.*
>
> **— JOHN 3:17**

I used to believe that God didn't really like me. I thought that my sinful thoughts and actions were so disgusting to him that he was allergic to me. I figured that Jesus's blood was like an antihistamine that would control the Father's reactions, making me more tolerable. But this is all non-sense. God loves us more than we can ever imagine, and he came in human form to rescue us and set us all free from these sorts of horrible lies–forever.

# 42 | A Never-Giving-Up Love

> *The LORD appeared to us in the past, saying:*
> *"I have loved you with an everlasting love;*
> *I have drawn you with unfailing kindness."*
>
> **— JEREMIAH 31:3**

The Father's great love for us is a constant thread woven throughout scripture. Sure, we screw up, we break precious things, and we might not deserve his care or attention, but God never gives up on us. He knows that his love will change us, set us free from our self-destruction, and rehabilitate his divine image within us. Like a painter restoring a precious work of art, the Father gently calls forth our original colors, lines, and hues.

# 43 | Letting Your Heart Be Moved

> *When he saw the crowds, he had compassion*
> *on them, because they were harassed and helpless,*
> *like sheep without a shepherd.*
>
> **— MATTHEW 9:36**

Many of us grew up with images of masculinity that were stoic and unmovable: the cowboy, the policeman, the firefighter. Some of our fathers and grandfathers were not emotional men, so compassion and gentleness weren't encouraged. Jesus shows us a new kind of godly masculinity: He let his heart be moved. When he saw people in need, it impacted him, and he responded with kindness. We're allowed to be men like this, too.

## 44 | Communities of Care

> *Walk with the wise and become wise,*
> *for a companion of fools suffers harm.*
>
> **— PROVERBS 13:20**

We sometimes find ourselves in the company of people who trigger our traumas, draw out the worst behaviors in us, demean us, or just don't inspire or encourage us. Sometimes they're friends from an earlier period of life. Often, they are drawn to us because of the peace and stability that we carry, and caring for them is good and right. But it's prudent to surround yourself with wise, loving, passionate, peaceful people–to create a community of others who build you up and encourage you.

## 45 | No Room for Revenge

> *Do not seek revenge or bear a grudge against*
> *anyone among your people, but love*
> *your neighbor as yourself. I am the LORD.*
>
> **— LEVITICUS 19:18**

Of all the appeals God makes, to not seek revenge or bear a grudge must be one of the most countercultural. We gorge ourselves on films and books that center on revenge, and we feel incredible satisfaction when someone gets what is coming to them. This thirst for justice is part of the divine image within us, but we delude ourselves if we think revenge is how justice works. Loving others and showing compassion is the path to true justice.

# 46 | Breaking Racial Barriers

> *For there is no difference between Jew and Gentile—the same Lord is Lord of all and richly blesses all who call on him.*
>
> **— ROMANS 10:12**

The world that Jesus grew up in was racially, religiously, and socially divided. The Jews were desperate for a savior who would defeat their enemies and promote their ethnic separateness. Jesus did neither. He invited everyone to him and declared them all his people. To make him Lord of your life requires that you submit everything to him. Looking down on others because of race, skin color, or ethnic background is utterly contrary to the way of Jesus.

# 47 | Regarding Foreigners and Refugees

> *Do not mistreat or oppress a foreigner, for you were foreigners in Egypt.*
>
> **— EXODUS 22:21**

When God became a human, he arrived in the body of a poor brown-skinned Jewish man living in a nation oppressed by a powerful empire. As a child, Jesus's family fled to Egypt and sought asylum there. Over the centuries, the dominant culture has appropriated this Jesus and turned him into a blue-eyed, blond-haired, white, Christian majority leader. For people of privilege to look down on refugees or foreigners is to reject God and to play the role of the oppressive ruler (who likes to kill children, by the way).

## 48 | Impossible Ways

> *See, I am doing a new thing! Now it springs up;*
> *do you not perceive it? I am making a way*
> *in the wilderness and streams in the wasteland.*

**— ISAIAH 43:19**

The ways of God can seem very difficult to us. The standard of love he models, the trust and faith required of us—it can all seem impossible. Yet here he is, making streams in the desert, giving us everything we need for life and love. What wilderness are you crossing right now? What miracles do you need to keep going? God knows your situation, and he is faithful to provide. Wait and watch.

## 49 | Shelter in Hard Times

> *Whoever dwells in the shelter of the Most High will rest*
> *in the shadow of the Almighty. I will say of the LORD, "He*
> *is my refuge and my fortress, my God, in whom I trust."*

**— PSALM 91:1-2**

I have lived through some epic storms in my life. I imagine you have as well. I hope that you knew the shelter and protection of God during those times. If you're going through a tumultuous season at present, I pray that you will find rest in the shelter of the Almighty, who invites you to come in and warm yourself on his breast.

# 50 | A Better Law of Love

> *Jesus replied: "'Love the Lord your God with all your heart and with all your soul and with all your mind.' This is the first and greatest commandment. And the second is like it: 'Love your neighbor as yourself.' All the Law and the Prophets hang on these two commandments."*
>
> **— MATTHEW 22:37-40**

When a ship at sea makes a fifteen-degree correction, it seems a small thing. Once that ship reaches the other side of the ocean, however, it's a huge difference. In the Hebrew scriptures, God provided all kinds of moral codes, some of which seem strange to us today. At the time, however, they helped guide a brutal Bronze Age culture a little closer toward love. Jesus explained that the Ten Commandments—and everything else—can be boiled down to just two foundational principles: Love God with everything you've got, and love your neighbor as if they were yourself. You can't lie, steal, cheat, or live selfishly if you are following the better law of love.

## Live Out the Word

In what ways have you been legalistic about following the rules?

What behaviors in your life couldn't really be described as loving?

How might your life change if you dropped all other religious behavior and focused on just these two commandments?

## 51 | Strength in God

*Finally, be strong in the Lord and in his mighty power.*

**— EPHESIANS 6:10**

Almost universally, men are expected to be strong and courageous. But what if you're not that kind of guy? What if your
body is small and frail? What if your mind is riddled with
fear? Growing up as an uncoordinated, sarcastic bookworm
in the hypermasculine, sports-obsessed culture of New
Zealand, I know what it's like to not feel strong or manly.
But God doesn't need me to be strong; he welcomes me
to rely on his mighty power. We can all develop strength of
trust and faith in the power of God.

## 52 | The Holy Spirit Guides Us

*And I will put my Spirit in you and move you to follow
my decrees and be careful to keep my laws.*

**— EZEKIEL 36:27**

Not only did Jesus simplify the list of laws and commandments, centering them on love, he also gave us his Spirit to
do the heavy lifting for us. Love is hard. At the best of times,
it asks a lot of us, and it frequently means laying down our
desires for the sake of others. What a blessing it is that the
very Spirit of God, who lays down his life for all, would come
and live inside us.

# 53 | Just Ask

*If you then, though you are evil, know how to give good gifts to your children, how much more will your Father in heaven give the Holy Spirit to those who ask him!*

**— LUKE 11:13**

Men have a reputation for not asking for help, especially when it comes to directions. I am guilty of this. I am happy to read instructions privately, but to expose my ignorance and put myself at the mercy of others to help me, provide for me, guide me? Ugh, I can't stand it. Yet I often need help, and God has provided a helper. We only need to ask.

# 54 | A Communal Project

*Therefore encourage one another and build each other up, just as in fact you are doing.*

**— 1 THESSALONIANS 5:11**

Another thing men often have a reputation for is going it alone. I don't think most of us naturally want to be alone; it's a survival tactic we learned after being rejected, hurt, or let down. For others, it's an issue of performance and achievement, the desire to prove themselves against some standard or goal. But real life happens in communities of people, not alone. Learning to love is a group project, and we need to encourage and support one another as brothers.

## 55 | Check Your Angle

> *As iron sharpens iron, so one person sharpens another.*
>
> **— PROVERBS 27:17**

As chunks of rock fall into a stream, they jostle one another, and their rough edges are slowly chipped off. The smooth pebbles you find in a river today are the result of decades those rocks have spent together. Human community works the same way, drawing us into collisions with one another that hopefully result in everyone becoming a little smoother, a little kinder, a little more tolerant. But the process can be painful. Iron will only sharpen iron if it's held at the correct angle; otherwise, it causes damage.

## 56 | The Team and Their Coach

> *For where two or three gather in my name, there am I with them.*
>
> **— MATTHEW 18:20**

God's Spirit is always with us, whether we're alone or with others, but something dynamic and mysterious happens when the Spirit of God in you reaches out to the Spirit of God in me. God seems to be drawn to our awkward attempts at relating to one another, at growing together and pursuing righteousness, of blessing our neighborhoods as one. The Father, Son, and Spirit are a community of love, after all. Next time you gather, keep an eye out for what the Spirit is doing.

## 57 | Never Rejected or Alone

> *For he has not despised or scorned the suffering*
> *of the afflicted one; he has not hidden his*
> *face from him but has listened to his cry for help.*
>
> **— PSALM 22:24**

We can survive truly terrible hardships, but to face them alone or to feel rejected while also suffering physical pain is often too much to bear. Here is a promise worth standing on: In the midst of every painful thing we endure, the Father hears us and does not ridicule us or hide his face from us. He listens to our cries for help and reaches out with care and comfort.

## 58 | Known as a Friend

> *I am the good shepherd; I know my sheep*
> *and my sheep know me.*
>
> **— JOHN 10:14**

In ancient times, shepherds weren't the industrial farmers we think of today, with large fenced-in fields or paddocks and flocks numbering in the hundreds and thousands. Shepherds knew each sheep individually, and the sheep could, in turn, recognize and follow their shepherd's voice. Some people relate to God like he's a modern industrial farmer, a distant owner they are vaguely aware of who exploits their body's productivity. But that is not the kind of relationship God wants with any of us. That's not really a relationship at all. I'd much rather be friends.

# 59 | The Defenders

*Learn to do right; seek justice. Defend the oppressed. Take up the cause of the fatherless; plead the case of the widow.*

**— ISAIAH 1:17**

There have been countless men throughout history who have been remarkable defenders of the oppressed—William Wilberforce, Mahatma Gandhi, Martin Luther King, Jr., to name a few. Unfortunately, these pioneers were opposed by vast numbers of other men (now nameless and forgotten) who made up a prevailing culture happy to exploit and dominate others. That culture is still with us. What kind of world might we and our partners and children enjoy if more of us defended the oppressed?

# 60 | Hate—Not Love—Is Blind

*But anyone who hates a brother or sister is in the darkness and walks around in the darkness.*

**— 1 JOHN 2:11**

Is there anyone in your life you really don't like? I mean, genuinely despise? Bad drivers, fans of an opposing team, and political enemies might be a starting point. What about the boss who ridiculed you, the teacher who abused you, or the pastor who manipulated you? Hatred may arise due to real injustice, but it is a powerful, blinding bondage that we must learn to get free from, lest we be consumed by resentment.

# 61 | A New, Softer Heart

> *I will give you a new heart and put a new spirit in you; I will remove from you your heart of stone and give you a heart of flesh.*
>
> **— EZEKIEL 36:26**

There's no shame in having a hard heart; life can be brutal and much of male culture promotes the idea that real men are hard men. But there's no future in that. To build lasting relationships, to raise a family, to respond with compassion to a hurting world, we need soft hearts. Thankfully, this is a surgery God performs himself. We don't have to force it; our part is simply to surrender to his hands as he operates.

# 62 | Hopeful Knowledge

> *I run in the path of your commands, for you have broadened my understanding. Teach me, LORD, the way of your decrees, that I may follow it to the end.*
>
> **— PSALM 119:32-33**

I didn't love school as a kid. I don't know if many from my generation did, taught as we were by old-school disciplinarians and hard taskmasters. But God is not that kind of teacher. While all new knowledge can be a little scary at first, when God broadens our understanding, it is always liberating and hopeful. A life spent in faithful learning at the feet of Jesus will appear to onlookers like scandalous grace.

## 63 | Life beyond Fear

> *The mind governed by the flesh is death, but the mind governed by the Spirit is life and peace.*
>
> **— ROMANS 8:6**

The flesh spoken of here is not your physical body. Your cells and atoms are not evil; they are holy creations of God. Without your body, you're nothing! But the body endures much pain and fear. A body that's riddled with fear and feels alone tends to look out for number one at the expense of all others. It is this system of egocentric self-protection that leads to death. To find lasting life and peace, we must lay our fear on the altar of the Spirit.

## 64 | Everything We Need

> *Do not worry, saying, "What shall we eat?" or "What shall we drink?" or "What shall we wear?" For the pagans run after all these things, and your heavenly Father knows that you need them. But seek first his kingdom and his righteousness, and all these things will be given to you as well.*
>
> **— MATTHEW 6:31-33**

Clothing and food are the basics of human survival. They can also become objects of obsessive pursuit and pride. I love that God doesn't shame us for needing them. He knows our situation and invites us to pursue him with abandon, trusting that he will provide everything we need.

# 65 | In Good Company

> *Better a dry crust with peace and quiet than a house full of feasting, with strife.*
>
> **— PROVERBS 17:1**

This proverb presents a truth similar to the one from yesterday but approaches it from a different angle. You can have all the good food, wine, and clothing you like, but if that's all you've pursued, then you won't have good company to enjoy it with. The more we allow God to reign over our lives, relationships, and families, the more we will experience his kingdom of peace, hope, and love.

# 66 | Where Is the Heart That Loves God?

> *But the LORD said to Samuel, "Do not consider his appearance or his height, for I have rejected him. The LORD does not look at the things people look at. People look at the outward appearance, but the LORD looks at the heart."*
>
> **— 1 SAMUEL 16:7**

Israel had chosen Saul—who stood head and shoulders taller than any other man—to be their first king. Sadly, he proved to be a poor choice. In discerning his successor, the prophet Samuel looked for height once again, until God invited him to think differently. Where is the heart that loves God and pursues his kingdom before all else? Is it yours?

## 67 | Better than Obedience

> *Again, the kingdom of heaven is like a merchant looking for fine pearls. When he found one of great value, he went away and sold everything he had and bought it.*
>
> **— MATTHEW 13:45–46**

An immature and hard-hearted man follows God begrudgingly. Obedience feels costly to him. When he captures a vision of what God and his kingdom are really like, however, he wants it no matter the cost. The aim of the game is freedom to pursue God out of your own desire, not out of religious compulsion. If you're not there yet, that's okay. Trust the Spirit to keep working on you.

## 68 | On Your Way to a Turning Point

> *Teach me knowledge and good judgment, for I trust your commands. Before I was afflicted I went astray, but now I obey your word.*
>
> **— PSALM 119:66–67**

The psalmist presents his time of affliction—a period of suffering resulting from having made poor choices—as the turning point in his life. Much of modern Christian culture is so obsessed with avoiding sin that sin has been robbed of any usefulness. Our missteps are the very thing that humble us and draw us back to God. We can be thankful that he is always bringing good out of bad, whether it's our own fault or not.

# 69 | Long-Term Plans

*"For I know the plans I have for you," declares the
LORD, "plans to prosper you and not
to harm you, plans to give you hope and a future."*

**— JEREMIAH 29:11**

Over a period of some four hundred years, Israel endured
a civil war and split into two nations, which were then
conquered by Assyria, Egypt, and Babylon. The temple in
Jerusalem was destroyed and the surviving population
exiled to foreign lands. The most popular inspirational Bible
verse, printed on mugs and greeting cards everywhere, was
written in the midst of horrific suffering preceding seventy
years of captivity. If that feels heavy, it's because it is—but
that's why the promise matters.

# 70 | The Face of Peace

*The LORD bless you and keep you; the LORD make
his face shine on you and be gracious to you; the LORD
turn his face toward you and give you peace.*

**— NUMBERS 6:24-26**

Right before this verse, God had instructed Moses that if
any of the Israelites wanted to make a vow of dedication,
they could follow a special rule and become a Nazirite.
Then God told Moses how his brother Aaron (the high priest)
should bless people—not just the vow-makers but everyone.
God cares that you get properly blessed. May this blessing be yours as well. May you know the face of God and
have peace.

# 71 | Doing Good

> *You know what has happened… how God anointed*
> *Jesus of Nazareth with the Holy Spirit*
> *and power, and how he went around doing good*
> *and healing all who were under the*
> *power of the devil, because God was with him.*
>
> **— ACTS 10:37A–38**

I love how Luke sums up the ministry of Jesus in Acts. He doesn't say Jesus's ministry was preaching repentance or teaching truth or correcting sinners. He says it was doing good and healing the sick. And why does Luke say this happened? Because God was with Jesus and had anointed him with the Holy Spirit. We need Jesus to come and do this for us. We're invited to do good, too.

# 72 | When to Walk Away

> *The news about him spread all the more,*
> *so that crowds of people came to hear him and to*
> *be healed of their sicknesses. But Jesus*
> *often withdrew to lonely places and prayed.*
>
> **— LUKE 5:15–16**

Jesus cared for everyone he met. He listened to their stories, healed their sicknesses, and mended their broken hearts. At the same time, he also knew when to walk away. Jesus knew his best work came from a place of rest and prayer, so he put a boundary in place to protect that. Boundaries aren't selfish or weak; they enable us to do our most meaningful work to the best of our abilities.

## 73 | Knowing Stillness

*He says, "Be still, and know that I am God; I will be
exalted among the nations, I will be exalted in the earth."*

**— PSALM 46:10**

The work of the gospel can consume us with busyness. We
might start with a pure-hearted desire for others to know
God, but the ever-present influence of post-industrial
capitalism can turn our religious work into an idol itself. To
deliver us from the toxicity of a frenetic lifestyle, God invites
us to be still and do nothing for him. Try sitting in total
silence for five minutes this morning, and consider that if
you do nothing, God will still be exalted.

## 74 | Why Does He Hide?

*Truly you are a God who has been hiding
himself, the God and Savior of Israel.*

**— ISAIAH 45:15**

I've definitely experienced times when God seems hidden
from me, when I feel alone and my prayers don't seem to
accomplish anything. These seasons can be very discour-
aging, but I have learned that this is often when God is
closest to us. We can't see him because he's right here, too
close for our eyes to focus on. This is where silent prayer
and stillness can help. If you are very quiet and shut out the
noise of the world, you just might hear God breathing.

## 75 | So That We Would Seek Him

*It is the glory of God to conceal a matter; to search out a matter is the glory of kings.*

**— PROVERBS 25:2**

God hides himself so that we can enjoy the thrill of the chase, the learning and the yearning that come with pursuit. By hiding clues about himself in scripture and concealing his hand in our lives, God sets up a grand game of hide-and-seek. His goal is to be found.

## 76 | Spirit-Infused Boldness

*After they prayed, the place where they were meeting was shaken. And they were all filled with the Holy Spirit and spoke the word of God boldly.*

**— ACTS 4:31**

After Jesus was raised from the dead and returned to the Father, the Holy Spirit filled his followers. In the face of murderous persecution, they were given boldness to tell everyone about Jesus and how he saved even the ones who killed him. Have you ever experienced this kind of courage? It comes from spending time with Jesus, and it's not given to proselytize or win arguments but to leave peace, joy, and wholeness in our wake.

## 77 | Deliverance and Thanksgiving

*The Lᴏʀᴅ is my strength and my defense; he has become my salvation. He is my God, and I will praise him, my father's God, and I will exalt him.*

**— EXODUS 15:2**

Standing on the seashore, the Israelites had just watched God deliver them from the Egyptian army, sweeping the Egyptian chariots and soldiers away into the waters. Whatever oppresses you, whatever keeps you captive, the Lord God is your defense and your salvation. If the day of your deliverance has not yet come, remain faithful and wait on the Lord. He knows and he cares. Whether you're still waiting or already celebrating, exalt and praise the Lord!

## 78 | Perspectives of Grace

*Now if we are children, then we are heirs—heirs of God and co-heirs with Christ, if indeed we share in his sufferings in order that we may also share in his glory. I consider that our present sufferings are not worth comparing with the glory that will be revealed in us.*

**— ROMANS 8:17–18**

Taking up your cross and loving others the way Jesus did is painful. It's also the invitation to be seen and known as God's own family. That's a remarkable privilege, and it comes with benefits. We are heirs to the kingdom of God; whatever Jesus inherits from his Father is ours, too.

## 79 | No Shame for Anxiety

> *When anxiety was great within me,*
> *your consolation brought me joy.*
>
> **— PSALM 94:19**

Anxiety is what we call fear that runs amok in our bodies
and minds. Basic fear is a good thing; it has kept you alive
thus far. But anxiety sickens us with a fear disproportionate
to our problems. It disconnects us from reality and leaves
us in the cold sweat of overwhelming panic. But God
doesn't shame us for our anxiety; he cares for us and con-
soles us. He knows the evil present in this life and how it
traumatizes us. On the other side of fear lies joy.

## 80 | Strength in Weakness

> *He said to me, "My grace is sufficient for you, for my*
> *power is made perfect in weakness." Therefore*
> *I will boast all the more gladly about my weaknesses,*
> *so that Christ's power may rest on me.*
> *That is why, for Christ's sake, I delight in weaknesses,*
> *in insults, in hardships, in persecutions,*
> *in difficulties. For when I am weak, then I am strong.*
>
> **— 2 CORINTHIANS 12:9–10**

I've experienced workplace burnout twice. I begged God
to heal my mind and calm my soul, and he asked, "What if I
didn't?" I realized I would have to rely on him for everything.
And perhaps that is the point. His strength might almost be
conditional on my weakness.

# 81 | An Honest Confession

> *Whoever conceals their sins does not prosper, but the one who confesses and renounces them finds mercy.*
>
> **— PROVERBS 28:13**

I think most of us are pretty familiar with the ways that we fall short of the mark and would rather not dwell on them, let alone share them with others. But things kept in the dark, like burdens carried alone, have a way of growing beyond our control. By honestly confessing our failures to a trusted brother in the Lord who won't shame us, we dismantle the hold that brokenness has over us. We then become aware that God's mercy was with us all along, never withheld.

# 82 | Mercy for Everyone

> *For God has bound everyone over to disobedience so that he may have mercy on them all.*
>
> **— ROMANS 11:32**

God holds up his standard of love, and every single one of us falls short. If God was like any other authority, that would be a problem; we would be punished or condemned, perhaps violently. Not so with God. The apostle Paul explains that God has let us all become stubbornly disobedient so that he can have mercy on everyone. Being a sinner is the very thing that qualifies you for God's grace and mercy! That's scandalously good news, and it should disarm our fear of punishment.

# 83 | No One Is Punished

*There is no fear in love. But perfect love drives out fear, because fear has to do with punishment. The one who fears is not made perfect in love.*

**— 1 JOHN 4:18**

Most modern human societies are built on the rule of law, which is upheld by the threat of violence. Your parents probably taught you similarly: Do bad things, and you get punished. The trouble is punishment is basically just revenge, so it doesn't fix the problem in our hearts. God looks at the heart, so when we do bad things, he simply forgives us, and this love begins to transform us from the inside out.

# 84 | Love Your Enemies

*You have heard that it was said, "Love your neighbor and hate your enemy." But I tell you, love your enemies and pray for those who persecute you, that you may be children of your Father in heaven.*

**— MATTHEW 5:43–45A**

What is God like? He loves everyone—whether they openly oppose him or just fall short of his standard of love. That includes you and me. The Father is unlike any parent or boss we've ever known; when we let him down, we have nothing to fear from him. He loves his enemies and invites us to learn to do the same. Why? Because love changes enemies into friends.

# 85 | The Wooing of the Human Mind

> *Once you were alienated from God and were enemies in your minds because of your evil behavior. But now he has reconciled you by Christ's physical body through death to present you holy in his sight, without blemish and free from accusation.*
>
> **— COLOSSIANS 1:21-22**

One of the natural consequences of broken behavior is that it darkens our sight and blinds us to reality. Sin taught us that God hated us, so we ran in terror. But it was never true. God loves us and has always been here within us. By becoming human, dying, and rising again, God defeated sin and death so our minds could accept his love.

# 86 | Nothing Can Separate Us

> *For I am convinced that neither death nor life, neither angels nor demons, neither the present nor the future, nor any powers, neither height nor depth, nor anything else in all creation, will be able to separate us from the love of God that is in Christ Jesus our Lord.*
>
> **— ROMANS 8:38-39**

Growing up, I was taught that sin separates us from God. The apostle Paul would disagree. What then do we say of sin? I believe it blinds us to the closeness of God's presence. We feel separated from God, so we act as if we were. But it's a lie. God is and has always been right here with you.

# 87 | Everything Is a Temple

*For in him all things were created: things in heaven and on earth, visible and invisible, whether thrones or powers or rulers or authorities; all things have been created through him and for him. He is before all things, and in him all things hold together.*

**— COLOSSIANS 1:16–17**

I know it can be hard to believe that God is present right now. There is always so much evidence to the contrary. The truth is, God is holding all the atoms of your body together, right now. He is present in everything. But he will feel far from us until we learn new ways of knowing, discerning, and being.

# 88 | Worthy of Our Devotion

*You alone are the LORD. You made the heavens, even the highest heavens, and all their starry host, the earth and all that is on it, the seas and all that is in them. You give life to everything, and the multitudes of heaven worship you.*

**— NEHEMIAH 9:6**

From the perfection of love between Father, Son, and Spirit, an idea was born: life. A universe, stars and planets, and a perfect blue ball teeming with all kinds of remarkable, beautiful creatures. We exist because God wanted us to. As you go about your day, pay attention to the world, and thank God for it. It's his love letter to you.

> *When all the people were being baptized, Jesus was baptized too. And as he was praying, heaven was opened, and the Holy Spirit descended on him in bodily form like a dove. And a voice came from heaven: "You are my Son, whom I love; with you I am well pleased."*
>
> **— LUKE 3:21–22**

Baptism is a ritual of death and rebirth. For Jesus, it was a prophetic picture of what would soon take place at the cross, where he would die so he could destroy death itself from within. For you and me, baptism is a statement we make that we are letting our old egocentric life die and are trusting God to raise up a new Jesus-centric life in us instead, a life that begins with these words: "You are my child. I love you. I am pleased with you."

## Live Out the Word

Have you been baptized? If so, reflect on the experience. What changed in your life?

Have you ever heard those words from your own parents? If not, can you offer them to yourself?

What would it mean for you to let your egocentric self die and to trust God to put a new life inside you, one in which you are not the center of the universe? Does this scare you? Why?

# 90 | A Better Foundation

*The rain came down, the streams rose, and the winds blew and beat against that house; yet it did not fall, because it had its foundation on the rock.*

**— MATTHEW 7:25**

Culture and society offer any number of possible foundations for us to build our lives and families on. Career, education, health and fitness, celebrity, wealth, and even military service are each trusted by different people as the foundation of a fulfilling life. It may be countercultural and even your closest friends and family may not understand, but trusting God and listening to his guidance is a far better foundation for your life than any of these worldly pursuits.

# 91 | A Restful Teacher

*Come to me, all you who are weary and burdened, and I will give you rest. Take my yoke upon you and learn from me, for I am gentle and humble in heart, and you will find rest for your souls. For my yoke is easy and my burden is light.*

**— MATTHEW 11:28-30**

How a Jewish rabbi interpreted and taught the Torah (the first five books of the Hebrew scriptures) was called his "yoke." Jesus's yoke is easy, and he offers reprieve for all those tired of saving their own lives. If the death of your egocentric life scares you, that's understandable, but you can trust Jesus with your future.

## 92 | Fearful by Default

> *When the people saw the thunder and lightning and heard the trumpet and saw the mountain in smoke, they trembled with fear. They stayed at a distance and said to Moses, "Speak to us yourself and we will listen. But do not have God speak to us or we will die."*
>
> **— EXODUS 20:18–19**

Israel's need for appointed priests arose because the populace was too scared of God to have a face-to-face relationship with him. Given our frail form and our many temptations, it's understandable that we fear God. Graciously, he works around our fear, accommodating it. God is not a danger to us; he is only a danger to our self-centeredness.

## 93 | The Law Was Fitted to Us

> *For the law was given through Moses; grace and truth came through Jesus Christ.*
>
> **— JOHN 1:17**

The Israelites' fear of God, coupled with their violent obsession with sacrifice, resulted in a complex system of laws and moral codes. God gave them this law to satisfy their need for it, not his. The law was fit to human parameters, to correct our course in a way we could understand. But it was never God's full intent. How can we know that? Because Jesus came in a human body and showed us what God is really like: boundless love, endless grace, and a light burden.

# 94 | Sacrifices Don't Work

> *The law is only a shadow of the good things that are coming—not the realities themselves. For this reason it can never, by the same sacrifices repeated endlessly year after year, make perfect those who draw near to worship.*
>
> **— HEBREWS 10:1**

Ever since humans could walk and hunt, we have been trying to earn the favor of our gods through sacrifice. But here is the shocking, scandalous truth at the heart of the gospel of grace: Sacrifices don't work and aren't necessary. We've always had the favor of God because he cares for his children. We are made perfect by his gift of life to us.

# 95 | Now We Can Ask for Help

> *I lift up my eyes to the mountains— where does my help come from? My help comes from the LORD, the Maker of heaven and earth.*
>
> **— PSALM 121:1-2**

Being self-sufficient is great if you hate asking for help, but it's not a sustainable way to live. To move beyond self-centeredness into trust and grace, you'll need support. This can be uncomfortable, but it's part of the journey toward communal life with God and others. We can look to the mountain, the same place we once feared, and ask God for help. Helping us is not a burden to him; he delights in it.

# 96 | One Family under God

> *Do we not all have one Father? Did not one God*
> *create us? Why do we profane the covenant*
> *of our ancestors by being unfaithful to one another?*
>
> **— MALACHI 2:10**

Many of us were taught to be self-sufficient and never rely on anyone but ourselves. This was one of the core tenets of the masculinity I was raised with—not by my parents, mind you, but by the wider cultural system. Others of us were taught to only trust people in our group and to fear or hate anyone from the outside. But all of this is unhelpful. With God as our father, all humanity is one family.

# 97 | One Body in Christ

> *In Christ we, though many, form one body, and each*
> *member belongs to all the others.*
>
> **— ROMANS 12:5**

Not only are we all part of God's family, but, in Jesus, we are even closer to one another than that: We are one body! Each of us has distinctive roles to play, and no part is more important than another. Furthermore, what happens to one part affects all the others, and we are called to care for and nurture other people as if they were as valuable to us as ourselves. If you let it, the Holy Spirit will move your thinking and being toward an embodied community life.

## 98 | Embrace the Mystery

*As you do not know the path of the wind, or how the body is formed in a mother's womb, so you cannot understand the work of God, the Maker of all things.*

**— ECCLESIASTES 11:5**

This is not an exclusively masculine trait, but many men love to figure out how things work. I'm in this camp, too; I've repaired all manner of appliances in my house by taking them apart and figuring them out. People are a bit harder to comprehend of course, and God is the greatest riddle of them all. Somehow, our loving, ever-present Creator is both knowable and an enigma never to be understood.

## 99 | Secrets Meant to Be Shared

*For who knows a person's thoughts except their own spirit within them? In the same way no one knows the thoughts of God except the Spirit of God.*

**— 1 CORINTHIANS 2:11**

Although the fullness of God may remain beyond what we can grasp, God longs to reveal himself to us. If you've been in a long-term relationship, you know what this is like. You meet someone, you fall in love, and then you spend the next ten years learning who they really are. The Holy Spirit does this, too, revealing God's thoughts and his ways to us, little by little, day by day. It takes time.

# 100 | Living Flames of Love

> *This is how love is made complete among us
> so that we will have confidence on the day of
> judgment: In this world we are like Jesus.*
>
> **— 1 JOHN 4:17**

As the Spirit reveals more of God to us, we should find ourselves becoming more and more like Jesus. What's often difficult for us is that this process is not something we can force or optimize or hurry. It's not a matter of mastering a spiritual discipline or winning a prize but of submitting ourselves to the refining fire of God's love. As we do this, we become living flames of love for the sake of the hurting world around us.

# 101 | Do No Harm

> *Love does no harm to a neighbor. Therefore love
> is the fulfillment of the law.*
>
> **— ROMANS 13:10**

You know the rules: Do not commit adultery, do not murder, do not steal, do not covet the possessions of your neighbor, and so on and so forth. There are quite a few of them, and here they are summed up simply by saying, "Do no harm." That is what God is like: He does no harm. He gives life, joy, peace, and hope. How much harm do you cause the people around you? Be honest. Ask them, even. The more you lean into Jesus, the less harm you will cause.

# 102 | Own Your Stuff

> *When anyone becomes aware that they
> are guilty in any of these matters, they must
> confess in what way they have sinned.*
>
> **– LEVITICUS 5:5**

What did you find out yesterday about the harm you cause?
Were you relieved or troubled? The fact is, we all cause harm.
The question is, what will we do about it? Will we man up
and own what we've done, confess our failures, and change
our ways? Or will we double down on self-protective pride,
blame others, and refuse to accept responsibility? One way
leads to personal growth and mutual thriving; the other leads
to continued bondage and darkness. The choice is yours.

# 103 | Reframing Sin

> *Indeed, there is no one on earth who is righteous,
> no one who does what is right and never sins.*
>
> **– ECCLESIASTES 7:20**

Why do we sin? I don't think it's because of a curse we
inherited from Adam and Eve. I believe it's because we're
vulnerable to harm. The self-centered things we do to
manage the pain of human life and preserve ourselves
typically come at the expense of others–and ourselves in the
long run. Sin is essentially collateral damage, a symptom of
our frailty and brokenness. God's response is for Jesus to
transform death into something we need not fear anymore
and to cleanse us of the dehumanizing consequences of
our brokenness.

# 104 | Free to Live in Love

> *What shall we say, then? Shall we go on sinning so that grace may increase? By no means! We are those who have died to sin; how can we live in it any longer?*
>
> **— ROMANS 6:1-2**

Because Jesus has defeated death, cleansed us of sin, and given us his Holy Spirit, the darkness has no hold on us anymore. There is no excuse for continuing to live in fear, protecting ourselves at the expense of others, and causing harm. That is an immature way to live. Jesus freed us from the fear of death and punishment. We are free to live in love and to give it away.

# 105 | Meeting Needs Poorly

> *Put to death, therefore, whatever belongs to your earthly nature: sexual immorality, impurity, lust, evil desires and greed, which is idolatry.*
>
> **— COLOSSIANS 3:5**

Why do we love food, sex, and money so much? Because they feel good! Living in these frail bodies, we are often desperate to feel anything other than lonely, afraid, or hungry. Lust and greed promise good feelings, instantly. The earthly nature is this system of quick, self-preserving comfort, which always comes at a cost to others. Living righteously is not ignoring your body and its needs but submitting them to God and trusting him to bring you fun and fulfillment.

# 106 | Relieved to Be Called a Sinner

> Here is a trustworthy saying that deserves full acceptance: Christ Jesus came into the world to save sinners—of whom I am the worst.
>
> **— 1 TIMOTHY 1:15**

Having taken on a human body and living in it for thirty years, Jesus understands the fears, pains, and temptations of human life. He gets what it is like to be us, and he doesn't shame us for the ways we fall short. But he does offer a different way, one that begins with honesty about our state and that entrusts all our fears to the care of the Father. It's really quite okay to be called a sinner.

# 107 | Poop and Grace

> He saved us, not because of righteous things we had done, but because of his mercy. He saved us through the washing of rebirth and renewal by the Holy Spirit.
>
> **— TITUS 3:5**

When a child poops in their diaper, you don't punish them for it. Despite how disgusting it is and what it will take for you to clean it up, it's natural for them, given their age and stage. That is how God sees us. He washes and renews us, and he gives us his Spirit to form us into maturity, where we might just poop on ourselves a little less.

# 108 | A Father Who Teaches

> *I gave an account of my ways and you answered me; teach me your decrees. Cause me to understand the way of your precepts, that I may meditate on your wonderful deeds.*
>
> **— PSALM 119:26–27**

As a kid, confessing my sins always felt so awkward. I was already embarrassed by what I had done, then I had to dredge it up in front of my parents and await whatever punishment they deemed fair. Not so with God. He knows punishment doesn't help, and that it's his love that molds us. He longs for us to turn toward home, admit our need, and embrace his process of restoration.

# 109 | Love and Patience

> *Love is patient, love is kind.*
>
> **— 1 CORINTHIANS 13:4A**

If we are to sit at the feet of God and learn what his way of love looks like, we can't do much better than the apostle Paul's treatise on love. Paul starts with patience and kindness, two core aspects of love. A man who loves well does not need to hurry others. A man who knows he is loved himself has fewer reasons to rush. Kindness hasn't always been accepted as a masculine trait in Western colonial culture, but it's high time we reclaimed it. Patience and kindness alone would go a long way toward transforming the world.

# 110 | Love and Pride

*It does not envy, it does not boast, it is not proud.*

**— 1 CORINTHIANS 13:4B**

Envy is the name of the emotion we feel when someone else has something that we also want. It makes us feel that there is something wrong with us, that if only we were different, we would also have that thing, that person, that job. Envy sows seeds of self-hatred, which is a form of self-centered pride because it sees itself as the ultimate cause of all possible problems. Self-hatred, flexing, and arrogant superiority are all incongruent with the others-centered way of love. Love always promotes and celebrates the worth and accomplishments of others.

# 111 | Love and Anger

*It does not dishonor others, it is not self-seeking,*
*it is not easily angered.*

**— 1 CORINTHIANS 13:5A**

Anger is one of the few emotions that has been celebrated in men. Being quick-tempered has often been synonymous with being a man of action. But anger, the feeling we get when we—or someone we care for—has been violated or blocked, cripples our ability to act rationally. Who can measure the harm that uncontrolled angry men have done in their families and beyond? Love serves others, cares for them, and does not seek its own betterment. Righteous anger at genuine injustice is anger that is slow enough to remain rational.

# 112 | Love and Forgiveness

> *It keeps no record of wrongs. Love does not delight in evil but rejoices with the truth.*
>
> **— 1 CORINTHIANS 13:5B–6**

When someone lets us down, it can be tempting to hold it over them, to keep a receipt and remind them of what they owe us. But this is a form of control and manipulation, which have nothing to do with love. Love does not fixate on people's errors but welcomes all into a community of forgiveness and reconciliation.

# 113 | Love Is Hard

> *It always protects, always trusts, always hopes, always perseveres.*
>
> **— 1 CORINTHIANS 13:7**

This final statement on love makes one thing very clear to me: It's impossible. I have tried so hard to always trust and to always hope, and I can't do it. I fall short of the way of love, which reveals something else: Love is from God. It's not something I can originate or perfectly emulate; it is something I can only participate in. I can enter into love and become a conduit for others to encounter it and find hope, protection, trust, and perseverance in the face of betrayal, loss, and every other kind of hardship. God is love.

# 114 | Love in Action

*Dear children, let us not love with words or speech*
*but with actions and in truth.*

**— 1 JOHN 3:18**

This is the invitation for all men who would be considered godly: to use our bodies and minds to serve others in love. To move from lip service to costly others-centered love and leave nothing but patience, kindness, truth, hope, and perseverance in our wake. To forever put away destructive anger, envy, selfish pride, manipulation, and obsession with self—in all its forms. This is what the way of love looks like, it's what Jesus showed us God is like, and it's what we're invited to reflect in our lives.

# 115 | A Constant Companion

*The LORD himself goes before you and will be*
*with you; he will never leave you nor forsake you.*
*Do not be afraid; do not be discouraged.*

**— DEUTERONOMY 31:8**

This call to love can feel like an impossible task, and it would be if not for God always being with us. Whatever the final outcome, we do not need to be discouraged or hopeless, for he will supply the love and guidance we need. We are never alone. He remains faithful.

# 116 | A Faithful Rock

*May your unfailing love be with us, Lord,*
*even as we put our hope in you.*

**— PSALM 33:22**

The Israelites were invited to be a blessing to the nations around them. They were the people God chose to demonstrate his love for all people. This way of love is countercultural enough in our day, but it was a seismic shift for them. They required an extensive list of rules to make any sense of it, and in the end, they couldn't work it out. But God remained faithful to the people he chose and to his plan of showing love to all. He will be faithful to you as well.

# 117 | A Champion of Hope and Freedom

*The Spirit of the Sovereign Lord is on me,*
*because the Lord has anointed me to proclaim good*
*news to the poor. He has sent me to bind up the*
*brokenhearted, to proclaim freedom for the captives*
*and release from darkness for the prisoners.*

**— ISAIAH 61:1**

Living outside the way of love isn't simply uncomfortable or painful; it leaves us trapped. We become captive to our own fears and the misguided actions they result in, as well as to the oppressive behavior of others. Jesus, God in human flesh, came to release us from all bondage, heal our wounds, and teach us how to live as agents of freedom.

## 118 | Gifts Are Better Than Payments

> *For the wages of sin is death, but the gift of God is eternal life in Christ Jesus our Lord.*
>
> **— ROMANS 6:23**

Wages are a familiar concept for us. When we work for someone, they owe us payment. If we screw up, we might owe them something back. It's easy to assume that God is transactional, too, so when we miss the mark of his righteousness, we expect some sort of punishment in return. But God is no punisher; as Creator and Lord of all, he is a giver. If sin was handing out our paychecks, it would say death on each one. Thankfully, God is a father, not a supervisor.

## 119 | New Life for All Creation

> *For as in Adam all die, so in Christ all will be made alive.*
>
> **— 1 CORINTHIANS 15:22**

Fear of death, the most natural animal instinct, is what drives the self-serving sin machine inside each of us. We are desperately afraid of our own frailty, and we will do almost anything to protect ourselves. Ironically, this path leads to the exact place we fear: death. Jesus displayed a new kind of humanity, one not ruled by fear of suffering or death. By defeating sin and death, Jesus unleashed a new kind of life that is relentlessly infecting and transforming all things. That's the good news of the gospel.

# 120 | Salvation Is Coming

> *I wait for the LORD, my whole being waits, and in his word I put my hope.*
>
> **— PSALM 130:5**

The pressures of this life are often relentless. I frequently find myself begging for rescue, crying out to Jesus for wisdom, guidance, patience, endurance . . . whatever I need to survive the current moment. This plea for rescue is not weakness; it is strength, and it has a long biblical tradition. The psalmist repeatedly lays out his situation before God, sparing no details of his struggle. Then he turns his gaze toward heaven and waits for the promise of salvation to be fulfilled. That's a good way to live.

# 121 | Tenacious Presence

> *To the roots of the mountains I sank down; the earth beneath barred me in forever. But you, LORD my God, brought my life up from the pit.*
>
> **— JONAH 2:6**

The brutal honesty found in the Psalms is found elsewhere in scripture as well. Depression? Check. Anxiety? Check. Suicidal ideation? Rejection? Losing your job? Loss of family relationships? Loss of health? All check. Every one of the most devastating experiences you might endure can be offered up to God without shame. He promises to be with us through everything we face. What's the worst thing in your life right now? How might it change if you could sense God's loving presence there (yes, even and especially there)?

# 122 | A Better Kind of Priest

> *Because Jesus lives forever, he has a permanent priesthood. Therefore he is able to save completely those who come to God through him, because he always lives to intercede for them.*
>
> **— HEBREWS 7:24B-25**

In the primordial past, when humans feared and worshipped all manner of gods, priests were appointed to stand in for the people and make requests of the fickle and angry gods on the people's behalf. Jesus established a new kind of priesthood founded on the truth that God is ever-present, ever-loving, and eager to visit with all his children. Jesus's life is now one of prayerful intercession that all would come to know his Father as he does.

# 123 | The Dawn of a New Era

> *He who was seated on the throne said, "I am making everything new!" Then he said, "Write this down, for these words are trustworthy and true."*
>
> **— REVELATION 21:5**

Jesus's insertion into human history is the point all creation pivots around. Everything before and after is different, or, at least, begins to be different. The capacity to live righteous lives, to overcome our fears and place our trust wholeheartedly in God, comes as a result of Jesus's incarnation, death, resurrection, and ascension. The gift of the Holy Spirit seals the deal. From that point on, humanity and all creation can learn to live a new way, one that reflects God.

# 124 | An Ever-Present, Living Witness

> *But the Advocate, the Holy Spirit, whom the Father will send in my name, will teach you all things and will remind you of everything I have said to you.*
>
> **— JOHN 14:26**

Coming up, we're going to look more closely at the life and teachings of Jesus. The important thing to remember as we do so is that Jesus's own Spirit is always available to us. The Holy Spirit reminds and informs us of all that Jesus did and is now doing in us so that we might participate in divine life. This is not to impress God or anyone else but so that we might live in love, continually transforming us and those around us.

# 125 | That None May Perish

> *For God so loved the world that he gave his one and only Son, that whoever believes in him shall not perish but have eternal life.*
>
> **— JOHN 3:16**

It is easy to miss the depths of beauty in this verse, the most famous verse in scripture. The gift of eternal life comes to us through Jesus. Jesus saves us from death having the last word over us. Jesus came because God loves us. He wasn't just a solution to a sin problem; he is a gift of love from God himself so we can live forever with God, like God. Every part of Jesus's life informs us of this and makes it possible.

## 126 | Humble Origins

> *My soul glorifies the Lord and my spirit rejoices*
> *in God my Savior, for he has been*
> *mindful of the humble state of his servant.*
>
> **— LUKE 1:46B–48A**

We can't talk about the life of Jesus without talking about his mother. Since she was young and unmarried Mary's pregnancy would have been scandalous in the misogynistic culture she lived in. Yet Mary accepted those risks with worship and joy, considering that God had looked favorably upon her. How many of us would praise God for allowing us to become the object of scandal? What a woman.

## 127 | God's Daughter

> *From now on all generations will call me blessed,*
> *for the Mighty One has done great things*
> *for me—holy is his name. His mercy extends to those*
> *who fear him, from generation to generation.*
>
> **— LUKE 1:48B–50**

Mary understood she was carrying the deliverance of her own people, Israel, and that all future generations would venerate her. For this, she praised God and declared his mercy. This must have required remarkable faith and character. God Almighty was conceived into human flesh and carried by this young, faithful girl. A man wasn't even involved in the process, which should probably help keep us humble.

## 128 | Birthed from a Prayer of Justice

*He has performed mighty deeds with his arm;*
*he has scattered those who are proud in*
*their inmost thoughts. He has brought down rulers*
*from their thrones but has lifted up the humble.*

**— LUKE 1:51–52**

Mary's courage is striking to me. Despite—or perhaps because of—her young age, she perceived the corruption of leaders, the empty religion of the proud, and the vanity of the mighty. Despite being a girl and not receiving a religious education, she knew the stories of God's faithfulness to her people. Women could only pray communally in the synagogue, yet here is pregnant Mary's prayer of justice, her voice standing alone, echoing through all time.

## 129 | The Queen of Heaven

*He has filled the hungry with good things but has sent*
*the rich away empty. He has helped his servant Israel,*
*remembering to be merciful to Abraham and his*
*descendants forever, just as he promised our ancestors.*

**— LUKE 1:53–55**

As a poor person, Mary knew what it was to be hungry. She knew what it was to feel her belly ache while seeing the rich carry themselves with opulence. She understood the injustice of this, and she knew God cared about it. Time itself was as pregnant as she was, ready for everything to change and the world to be made new. Thank God for Mary.

# 130 | Something Real

> *In him was life, and that life was the light*
> *of all mankind. The light shines in the darkness,*
> *and the darkness has not overcome it.*
>
> **— JOHN 1:4–5**

We lived in darkness for so long that it was easy to believe that we were beings of darkness, capable only of evil. Our brokenness often makes us feel like God is far away, not able to come near us. Yet here he comes in human flesh, penetrating our darkness to the core, looking on all of our sin without flinching. Darkness doesn't even exist, after all; it's simply the absence of light. Light comes and fills us up with something real and tangible: the present life of God.

# 131 | The Divine Human Candle

> *I have come into the world as a light, so that no one*
> *who believes in me should stay in darkness.*
>
> **— JOHN 12:46**

It's incredible to me that God chose to come in human form. He could have sent angels, used voices booming from the clouds, or just changed everything by snapping his fingers, but he didn't. He came as a man, walking and talking, drinking and eating, peeing and pooping–and teaching and modeling a way of life utterly contrary to any man before him. Ask yourself, are you a man just like other men before you? Do you fit the mold of manhood expected by society? Jesus sure didn't.

## 132 | The Golden Rule

*Do to others as you would have them do to you.*

**— LUKE 6:31**

Jesus grew up and began teaching, traveling from town to town around Judea and up to Jerusalem for feasts and other important occasions. Many of his teachings could be summed up in this, what has often been referred to as the Golden Rule: Do to others what you would have them do to you. It invites us to integrity of action, to contribute to the world only exactly what we would hope to find in it ourselves. I don't know about you, but I offer a lot more pessimism, complaining, and judgment than I want to receive. You?

## 133 | A Promise for the Downtrodden

*Blessed are the poor in spirit, for theirs is the kingdom of heaven.*

**— MATTHEW 5:3**

One of Jesus's most famous sermons took place on a hill in Galilee. Shortly after he was baptized and had fasted forty days in the desert, Jesus began to teach a value system that resonated strongly with the poor and oppressed people around him. Although the rich and powerful seem to have everything they want, Jesus explained that those who are downtrodden, depressed, and greatly burdened are the most blessed because God's kingdom is theirs. Have you experienced the royal fellowship of being poor in spirit?

# 134 | A Promise for the Grieving

> *Blessed are those who mourn, for they will be comforted.*
>
> **— MATTHEW 5:4**

Losing a dearly loved one, whether a friend, spouse, or child, is devastating. It clouds the rest of our lives and reshapes our reality into "before" and "after." Smaller losses cause grief no less real. Jesus said that those who are deeply grieved are the most blessed, for they are in line to be comforted by the Father himself. Far from a cold and distant God, our Father in heaven is a loving, intimate parent who's familiar with suffering and loss. Everything you are grieving today God understands. He offers his presence to support you.

# 135 | A Promise for the Meek

> *Blessed are the meek, for they will inherit the earth.*
>
> **— MATTHEW 5:5**

Show me a man who is meek, and I will show you a man who feels out of place in the male world. To be meek is to be righteous through patience, humility, and gentleness. It is to submit to others graciously and not demand your own way. Let's be clear: Meekness was not promoted as a male value in the world I grew up in. Meekness might even be the polar opposite of toxic masculinity. But Jesus said the entire earth belongs to those who submit to this way of love.

# 136 | A Promise for the Oppressed

> *Blessed are those who hunger and thirst for righteousness, for they will be filled.*
>
> **— MATTHEW 5:6**

Do you hunger and thirst for righteousness? Are you desperate for goodness and justice to flow within you and around you? I'd like these things, for sure, but I can't say I'm dying for them. Could that be because I have not been a victim of very much injustice? I believe these words resonate most with those who know what the heavy boot of oppression feels like. If you are greatly oppressed by evil, your guts will ache for a feast of righteousness. And Jesus promised you will be satisfied.

# 137 | A Promise for the Merciful

> *Blessed are the merciful, for they will be shown mercy.*
>
> **— MATTHEW 5:7**

To receive mercy is to be forgiven and let off the hook when we have wronged someone or to be rescued in a desperate time. Mercy is another one of those values that hasn't been seen as very masculine. A manly man gives people what they deserve, right? Unless that's not true. Jesus held up mercy as a picture of justice and beauty and said that those who are merciful will experience being shown mercy themselves. I, for one, would like to receive mercy when I need it, and I would prefer nothing stands in the way.

## 138 | A Promise for Those Pursuing Wholeness

> *Blessed are the pure in heart, for they will see God.*
>
> **— MATTHEW 5:8**

The invitation to be pure in heart used to make me feel ashamed because of my impure thoughts. Then I read Eugene Peterson's translation. The Message says you're blessed when you get your heart and mind put right, because then you can see God more clearly. Purity of heart is not a religious requirement that only the holiest priests achieve, it's the result of God healing us so we can see him. That's the birthright of every human.

## 139 | A Promise for the Peacemakers

> *Blessed are the peacemakers, for they will be called children of God.*
>
> **— MATTHEW 5:9**

In James Gunn's film *The Suicide Squad*, John Cena plays a brutal, muscle-bound vigilante called Peacemaker, who slaughters anyone who stands in the way of peace. The character of Peacemaker ridicules our ideas of redemptive violence and our love of powerful masculinity. Rather than doing any violence to us, Jesus brings peace by allowing us to kill him. The Son of God declares that all who enter into his way of co-suffering peacemaking shall be called children of God. Is your peace more like the Peacemaker's or Jesus Christ's?

## 140 | A Promise for the Persecuted

*Blessed are those who are persecuted because of righteousness, for theirs is the kingdom of heaven.*

**— MATTHEW 5:10**

Righteousness seems to provoke the wrath of both the religious and the powerful. Jesus calls those who die or are persecuted for righteousness "blessed." He promised them the kingdom of God. When this world is brutally unkind to you, take heart that a new life is springing up inside you.

## 141 | A Promise for the Unjustly Accused

*Blessed are you when people insult you, persecute you and falsely say all kinds of evil against you because of me.*

**— MATTHEW 5:11**

Jesus wraps up the Beatitudes (blessings) by identifying all of them with himself: "When you live the way I have taught you, people will lie about you and attack you. Your meekness will provoke them. Your burden of justice will drive them to slander you and murder you." Like his own mother you might be scandalized and villainized for nothing more than obedience to God. And for all of this, you are blessed. Welcome to the sacred company of Jesus.

# 142 | A Moment's Rest

> *Then, because so many people were coming and going that they did not even have a chance to eat, he said to them, "Come with me by yourselves to a quiet place and get some rest."*
>
> **— MARK 6:31**

Word of Jesus's teachings and miracles spread like wildfire. Very soon, Jesus and his friends were overwhelmed at the numbers, so at Jesus's instruction, they got into a boat to find a quiet place and catch a moment's rest. Read the whole chapter of Mark 6 to hear how rest didn't really play out but an incredible miracle did instead. Remember, rest is important even for those saving the world.

# 143 | A Higher Standard

> *But I tell you that anyone who looks at a woman lustfully has already committed adultery with her in his heart.*
>
> **— MATTHEW 5:28**

Jesus's followers knew their law stated that anyone who committed adultery be put to death by stoning–both parties. Remember that this law was built upon Bronze Age savagery; it was never the fullness of God's design. Jesus proved this by taking the rule even further, saying that adultery happens simply by lustful thought. How many times have you committed adultery this week? Thankfully, Jesus doesn't throw stones, as we shall see tomorrow.

# 144 | Those without Sin Do Not Throw Stones

> *Jesus straightened up and asked her, "Woman, where are they? Has no one condemned you?" "No one, sir," she said. "Then neither do I condemn you," Jesus declared. "Go now and leave your life of sin."*
>
> **— JOHN 8:10–11**

Jesus was near infamous for his mercy, so some religious leaders tried to trap him into violating the law about stoning adulterers. They caught a woman (But no man? Suspicious . . .) and dragged her to Jesus, who immediately saw through their hypocrisy. He cleverly invited whoever was sinless to go ahead and be the first to throw a stone. At this, the men gradually dispersed, as exposed and ashamed as the woman lying in the dust. Jesus—the only one worthy to throw stones—refused to, saving her life and erasing her shame.

## Live Out the Word

Have you ever been a victim of religious hypocrisy? What happened?

When have you judged and condemned others, throwing stones at sinners?

Are you a man who is safe for women, especially at their most vulnerable? What would it take for you to become a man like Jesus, who saves and frees a naked woman in the dust?

# 145 | Merciful Love for All

*Be merciful, just as your Father is merciful.*

**— LUKE 6:36**

In the Beatitudes, Jesus explained that those who are merciful will be shown mercy. This appeal would have encouraged those who hadn't been shown mercy lately. Shortly after, Jesus takes a different tone and simply charges his listeners, "Be merciful!" Why? Because God is merciful and we are made in his image, to be like him. That means it's actually in your true nature to be merciful; you've just forgotten how to be your true self. Drop the trappings of modern masculinity and return to your original design, that of a kind and generous giver who loves his enemies, showing mercy to all.

# 146 | Presence Never Withheld

*All those the Father gives me will come to me, and whoever comes to me I will never drive away.*

**— JOHN 6:37**

Jesus responded with compassionate attention to everyone who came to him. No one was rejected; each person was welcome and received something. When we are tempted to put up walls, to control access to ourselves and be stingy with our time and energy, Jesus shows us a different way. He gives of himself endlessly, trusting his Father to sustain him. It's important to develop healthy boundaries so we can care for others sustainably, but at the end of the day, I want to be this generous, too.

# 147 | An Endless Spring

*Jesus answered, "Everyone who drinks this water will be thirsty again, but whoever drinks the water I give them will never thirst. Indeed, the water I give them will become in them a spring of water welling up to eternal life."*

**— JOHN 4:13–14**

The life of God, full of peace, righteousness, and love, is always available to us. By turning toward Jesus and allowing his Spirit to flow in us, divine life bubbles up within. We don't have to strive or work hard to be good. Instead, we can allow the Holy Spirit to manifest its goodness in us. This is the living water Jesus offers to all who come to him.

# 148 | A Recipe for Blindness

*Why do you look at the speck of sawdust in your brother's eye and pay no attention to the plank in your own eye? . . . You hypocrite, first take the plank out of your own eye, and then you will see clearly to remove the speck from your brother's eye.*

**— MATTHEW 7:3, 5**

This famous passage reminds us of the importance of self-awareness. When we take issue with others, judgmentally nitpicking their mistakes without first dealing with our own, we aren't serving anybody well. How can we even hope to accurately discern the best path forward for a brother when our own steps are so wobbly? Jesus identifies self-awareness as an ingredient in loving others.

# 149 | Life through Death

> *Jesus answered, "Very truly I tell you, no one can enter the kingdom of God unless they are born of water and the Spirit. Flesh gives birth to flesh, but the Spirit gives birth to spirit."*
>
> **— JOHN 3:5-6**

Nothing about the kingdom of God, not the peace, love, hope, or freedom that comes from righteousness, can be reached by human effort. We can't white-knuckle our way to godliness or prove our worth by trying harder. We must die to our self-propelled ways and go down into the waters of death, trusting the Spirit of God to birth new life in us. This new life is God's life; it fears nothing and loves all.

# 150 | A Faithful Servant

> *Who then is the faithful and wise servant, whom the master has put in charge of the servants in his household to give them their food at the proper time? It will be good for that servant whose master finds him doing so when he returns.*
>
> **— MATTHEW 24:45-46**

When Jesus told this story, his audience would have included enslaved people, hired servants, and their masters. I suspect he is referring to himself as the chief servant. Like Jesus, a good and godly man is faithful with what has been entrusted to him. Whether that's your children, your employees, or the team you coach, nurturing them and caring for their needs is holy and righteous work.

## 151 | Love, Love, Love

> He answered, "'Love the Lord your God with
> all your heart and with all your soul and
> with all your strength and with all your mind';
> and, 'Love your neighbor as yourself.'"
>
> **— LUKE 10:27**

All the exhaustive commandments of the Hebrew scriptures as well as the scandalous grace of Jesus is summed up in this: Love God, love yourself, and love others. They're all intrinsically linked. Which of these is the hardest for you? For me, it was loving myself. I once dedicated a year to loving myself the way God loves me, and it changed my whole life.

## 152 | Hope over Hurt

> But everyone who hears these words of mine
> and does not put them into practice is like a foolish
> man who built his house on sand.
>
> **— MATTHEW 7:26**

Jesus was known as a gentle teacher, but still had strong words for self-righteous religious leaders. The hurting, who made up most of Jesus's audience, received hope and encouragement. That didn't stop Jesus from laying it out: If we ignore his words and do not follow his way of love, we'll end up living with the consequences. And I've already tasted enough foolishness for one lifetime.

## 153 | Even So . . .

> *If anyone hears my words but does not keep them, I do not judge that person. For I did not come to judge the world, but to save the world.*
>
> **— JOHN 12:47**

I love the playfulness in the Gospels. According to Matthew, Jesus says, "If you don't do what I say, you're foolish." John, likely writing some decades later, clarifies, "But even if you are foolish, I don't judge you for it." This is a big deal. Sitting over us in judgment, pointing out all the ways we fall short, doesn't solve anyone's problems, so God doesn't do it. Instead, he gets down on his knees in the muck with us and saves us from our foolishness.

## 154 | A God of Compassion and Sorrow

> *Jesus wept.*
>
> **— JOHN 11:35**

This is one of the most precious pieces of scripture to me. Standing in a crowd of mourners, grieving their brother and friend's untimely death, Jesus joins in the weeping. Even knowing he is going to resurrect Lazarus, Jesus lets grief flow through him. Our God is not so glorious that he is indifferent to human emotions. He is more glorious because he understands and cares about the tragedies that befall us. He knows what it's like to lose a loved one. Think of the hardest thing in your life right now and ask Jesus how he feels about it.

## 155 | Bigger Things

*And I, when I am lifted up from the earth,*
*will draw all people to myself.*

**— JOHN 12:32**

Most of Jesus's disciples were Jews. A few Romans and Samaritans pop up, but most people thought Jesus had come solely for the nation of Israel. Writing decades later, John gave Jesus language more inclusive of a wider audience. He was not just Israel's Messiah, after all; he is the Savior of the human race. And that word *draw*? The Greek is more like "drag." Jesus will *drag* the human race toward him.

## 156 | Ultimate Humility

*"No," said Peter, "you shall never wash my feet." Jesus*
*answered, "Unless I wash you, you have no part*
*with me." "Then, Lord," Simon Peter replied, "not just*
*my feet but my hands and my head as well!"*

**— JOHN 13:8–9**

The streets of most first-century cities were disgusting, filled with excrement, trash, and decay. Clad in little more than sandals, most people's feet were filthy. When guests entered the house of someone of means, a household servant or enslaved person might be made to wash their feet. Jesus takes on the ultimate act of cultural humility by washing his disciples' feet. Peter refuses at first, but then he understands.

## 157 | Much More than a Teacher

> *Jesus answered, "I am the way and the truth and the life. No one comes to the Father except through me."*
>
> **— JOHN 14:6**

Having spent at least three years together, Jesus and his disciples came up to Jerusalem once again to observe Passover. After washing their feet, he began a long speech, taking up chapters 13 to 17 in John's gospel. It's a bit like his last will and testament, his final chance to deposit what he wants his friends to know about the divine life. If they still only thought of him as a teacher, he blows their minds with this: "I am the way. I am the truth. I am the life."

## 158 | A Live-in Helper

> *And I will ask the Father, and he will give you another advocate to help you and be with you forever—the Spirit of truth.*
>
> **— JOHN 14:16–17A**

Far from just a prophet or a good man, Jesus is God himself made human. His humanity bonded to ours, and we were carried in his death, resurrection, and ascension to the Father. Jesus is life itself, the bread and the living water that holds all creation together. And as if that wasn't enough, he asked the Father to send his Spirit back to dwell within each of us. The Holy Spirit, who helps and advocates for us, is the same spirit Jesus had.

## 159 | A House Called Love

> *As the Father has loved me, so have I loved you.*
> *Now remain in my love.*
>
> **— JOHN 15:9**

If you're getting sick of the word *love*, I'm really sorry, but it's kind of the point. The challenge Jesus laid before his friends was to let everything he had done for them be enough and to simply remain in God's love. To not turn back to religious works, to not offer sacrifices to try to appease God, to not run from his wrath or any such nonsense. To remain in his love. What if you took up residence in the house called love and never left?

## 160 | It's Not Going to Be Easy

> *I have told you these things, so that in me you*
> *may have peace. In this world you will have trouble.*
> *But take heart! I have overcome the world.*
>
> **— JOHN 16:33**

This is another of my favorite pieces of scripture because it's so real. Jesus explains to his friends that everything he has said over the preceding hours is so that they may have peace in the hardships that are coming. Jesus doesn't promise an easy life; he literally promises trouble! But trouble surrounded by peace, shalom, harmonious co-existence. The Prince of Peace has overcome the world and its systems of oppression and invites you to live by the Spirit.

# 161 | Nothing Hidden

*Father, I want those you have given me to be
with me where I am, and to see my glory,
the glory you have given me because you loved me
before the creation of the world.*

**— JOHN 17:24**

To see something in its glory is to see it for all it really is. We use the figure of speech "saw them in all their glory" to refer to seeing someone naked, with nothing hidden. As the hour of Jesus's death draws near, he asks the Father that all his friends would have their eyes opened, that they would see him for who he really is. Do you have people who see you for who you really are?

# 162 | Returning to the Garden

*When he had finished praying, Jesus left with his
disciples and crossed the Kidron Valley.
On the other side there was a garden, and he and
his disciples went into it.*

**— JOHN 18:1**

Jewish prophecies spoke of Elijah returning and the Messiah coming, both via the Kidron Valley. The Revelation of John also depicts the great clash between God and the forces of evil taking place in the Kidron Valley. And so, Jesus crossed the Kidron with his friends to go to a garden to spend time with God, just like Adam and Eve, like humanity was always meant to. The rebirth of the entire cosmos was on its way.

## 163 | Taking All Our Pain

> *"My soul is overwhelmed with sorrow to the point of death," he said to them. "Stay here and keep watch."*
>
> **— MARK 14:34**

When traumatic things happen, our brains and bodies have a way of dissociating in order to push through. Rational thought goes offline, survival instincts kick in, and adrenaline overrides pain. Praying in the garden, Jesus was preparing to do something unheard of: He would pick up all the torment and brokenness of anyone who had lived or would ever live, and he would feel it all, remaining present to it so he could offer it up to his Father to be healed and cleansed. No wonder he sweat blood.

## 164 | Crucified for Our Sake

> *When they hurled their insults at him, he did not retaliate; when he suffered, he made no threats. Instead, he entrusted himself to him who judges justly. "He himself bore our sins" in his body on the cross, so that we might die to sins and live for righteousness; "by his wounds you have been healed."*
>
> **— 1 PETER 2:23-24**

Jesus was unjustly accused and did not defend himself. He was mocked, beaten, and scourged with a whip. Finally, after being forced to carry a wooden cross to the hill of Golgotha, he was crucified, willingly accepting this senseless violence to show us once and for all just how much God loves us.

## 165 | Heed the Call

> *Then Jesus said to his disciples, "Whoever*
> *wants to be my disciple must deny themselves*
> *and take up their cross and follow me."*
>
> **— MATTHEW 16:24**

You and I were made in God's image, to be like God. Jesus showed us what this means. We must lay down our lives, take up the burdens that God gives us to bear, and then follow Jesus in co-suffering love. That's the call. It's not for the faint of heart. True courage and strength are found in deprioritizing yourself and serving others. Jesus is the historical model for this as well as the living source of life we must tap into to make it possible in us.

## 166 | Second in Line

> *In their fright the women bowed down with their*
> *faces to the ground, but the men said to them,*
> *"Why do you look for the living among the dead?*
> *He is not here; he has risen!"*
>
> **— LUKE 24:5–6A**

When Jesus was crucified, most of his disciples fled and hid. Only his mother, John, and a few women stuck around to watch him die. After he was buried, it was the women once again who found the courage to go and visit his grave. They were first in line to meet the angels and see the risen Lord. Who are some of the brave women in your life who went before you and showed you the way?

# 167 | The Last Straw

> *So the other disciples told him, "We have seen the*
> *Lord!" But he said to them, "Unless I see the nail marks*
> *in his hands and put my finger where the nails*
> *were, and put my hand into his side, I will not believe."*

**— JOHN 20:25**

After being raised from the dead, Jesus appeared to some of his friends in the room they were hiding in. Sadly, Thomas wasn't there, and he missed the encounter. I find great solidarity in Thomas's unvarnished honesty. He couldn't risk having his heart broken once more. If you've had your hopes dashed again and again and you aren't sure you can hope anymore, Thomas, the disciple of Jesus, gets it.

# 168 | God Meets Us Where We're At

> *Then he said to Thomas, "Put your finger here; see*
> *my hands. Reach out your hand and put it*
> *into my side. Stop doubting and believe." Thomas*
> *said to him, "My Lord and my God!"*

**— JOHN 20:27-28**

Jesus meets Thomas on the terms he specified! Even in glory, Jesus models humility. And in being met right where he is, Thomas recognizes what no one else had quite figured out: Jesus is God! Standing right in front of them! If you were ever taught that you must come to God on his terms, Thomas proves otherwise.

# 169 | A New Kind of Life

*Now this is eternal life: that they know you, the only true God, and Jesus Christ, whom you have sent.*

**— JOHN 17:3**

Jesus opened the way to eternal life for all humanity, but what exactly is eternal life? At first glance, it's life that doesn't end, life that is no longer bound by death. But on closer examination, Jesus is explaining that eternal life is not just a matter of time but a new quality or kind of life. That new kind of life is defined by knowing God and Jesus, who showed us what God was like. That means eternal life is something that begins right now, not after we die.

# 170 | Spread the Word

*Therefore go and make disciples of all nations, baptizing them in the name of the Father and of the Son and of the Holy Spirit.*

**— MATTHEW 28:19**

The revolution that Jesus began wasn't just for the Jews or even for the Christians—it was for everyone! But how will they know what has happened if we don't tell them? Jesus commissioned his disciples to go and tell everyone everywhere about God's great love and what it means for them. That invitation continues. When you and I meet people, we can ask the Holy Spirit what good work God has been doing in their lives and share it when the time is right.

## 171 | Not Left Behind

> *And surely I am with you always,*
> *to the very end of the age.*
>
> **— MATTHEW 28:20B**

One of the names of Jesus was Emmanuel, which means "God with us." Many other passages of scripture speak of God living within us, God being present when two or three are gathered, and so on. Jesus blessed his disciples and assured them that he would be with them always. This is a great promise that we can rely on every day. Jesus, we need you. Jesus, we believe you are here. Jesus, open our eyes to see you and our ears to hear you. Emmanuel, make yourself real to us.

## 172 | The First Day of the Rest of Your Life

> *When he had led them out to the vicinity of Bethany,*
> *he lifted up his hands and blessed them.*
> *While he was blessing them, he left them and was*
> *taken up into heaven. Then they worshiped*
> *him and returned to Jerusalem with great joy.*
>
> **— LUKE 24:50–52**

At the time of Jesus, people believed the sky was blue because the floor of heaven was made of blue gemstones. We know a lot more about the sky now, so we are left with a sacred mystery: Jesus has departed; Jesus is always with us; Jesus will come again. However it happened, Jesus blessed his disciples and he offers blessing for you and me today.

# 173 | The Rock

> *There is no one holy like the LORD; there is no one*
> *besides you; there is no Rock like our God.*
>
> **— 1 SAMUEL 2:2**

I was raised in a Christian home and knew God from a young age. I've gone through periods of wrestling with my faith, of course, as most people have. Truly, I don't know where I would be today without God to lead me, hold me during times of distress, guide me toward wisdom, and call me higher to his way of love. Though I haven't always appreciated it, God has been my constant companion for over thirty years. Let God be a steadfast rock in your life.

# 174 | Rituals of Remembrance

> *But remember the LORD your God, for it is he who*
> *gives you the ability to produce wealth,*
> *and so confirms his covenant, which he swore to*
> *your ancestors, as it is today.*
>
> **— DEUTERONOMY 8:18**

In our digital, globalized world, it seems increasingly difficult to track the passage of time and remember what has happened in the past. God instructed the Israelites to stack stones, to celebrate feasts, to move into tents, and to do all manner of things to remember and commemorate what he had done for them. Does your family have any traditions or customs that you follow to remind yourselves of God's goodness to you? If not, could you create something?

# 175 | Generations of Faithfulness

> *No one will be able to stand against you all the days of your life. As I was with Moses, so I will be with you; I will never leave you nor forsake you.*
>
> **— JOSHUA 1:5**

I come from many generations of followers of Jesus, but I rarely think about the faith of my parents, grandparents, and beyond. God often uses the names of people's forebears in scripture to demonstrate his faithfulness. Whether you are like me or you're a first-generation Jesus follower, consider the ways that God has been faithful to humans in the past. He will be faithful to you as well. You stand in a long line of God's beloved.

# 176 | More than a Helping Hand

> *Look to the LORD and his strength; seek his face always.*
>
> **— 1 CHRONICLES 16:11**

I'm the eldest of three boys, and I'm always fascinated by my friends who don't have siblings—they are comfortable living alone, traveling solo, and doing their own thing in a way that I don't think I'll ever be. Whether you're someone who thoroughly enjoys your own company or you prefer being with others, you don't have to live from your own strength. Look to the Lord. Seek his face. God loves to lend a helping hand and so much more.

## 177 | Strong but Gentle

*In his hand is the life of every creature and
the breath of all mankind.*

**— JOB 12:10**

When I was eight years old, I accidentally drowned some ducklings. I found them in a cow trough on the farm where I lived, and for whatever reason, I pushed one under the water. It quickly bobbed back up to the surface, which I thought was cool, so I pushed them all down a few more times. Eventually, they stopped coming back up . . . and I ran home, scared and ashamed. The Creator of the universe holds all of us in his hands, and thankfully, he is far gentler than we could ever hope or imagine.

## 178 | Cleansed and Renewed

*Create in me a pure heart, O God, and
renew a steadfast spirit within me.*

**— PSALM 51:10**

I can surely relate to the psalmist's request for a pure heart. Can you? I've done so many things I'm not proud of, thought dark thoughts, and felt terrible feelings, as perhaps you have, too. We can all take great comfort in knowing God isn't shocked by any of it and doesn't hold anything against us. Better yet, he renews our hearts and minds, filling us with clean, pure light and giving his own spirit of faithful righteousness to dwell within us.

# 179 | Neither Slumber nor Sleep

*He will not let your foot slip—he who watches over you will not slumber; indeed, he who watches over Israel will neither slumber nor sleep.*

**— PSALM 121:3–4**

Whatever challenges or obstacles you are facing in your current season of life, may these words be a source of encouragement and hope to you. When the path seems slippery, God will steady your feet. When you lie down at night to rest, he will watch over you and stand guard. The Creator of the universe and Lover of all humanity watches over you day and night. May you experience that to be true for yourself.

# 180 | Plans of Redemption

*Like water spilled on the ground, which cannot be recovered, so we must die. But that is not what God desires; rather, he devises ways so that a banished person does not remain banished from him.*

**— 2 SAMUEL 14:14**

I used to worry a lot about the bad things I did, thinking they made me untouchable and revolting. As I grew to know God more, I learned that he doesn't want any of us to feel like we are banished or exiled from him. The things that have happened to us and the things we have done are no obstacle to him. He constantly thinks up more ways of restoring us and making us whole, returning us to the awareness of his presence.

# 181 | Finding Courage When We Need It

> *Be strong and courageous. Do not be afraid or terrified because of them, for the LORD your God goes with you; he will never leave you nor forsake you.*
>
> **— DEUTERONOMY 31:6**

Do you face any enemies—people who rob you of peace, threaten to hurt you or slander you or dishonor your dignity? I had a co-worker once who spent two years assassinating my character. It's horrible to have an enemy, but we don't need to live in fear of them. Place your trust in God, be honest about your suffering, and wait for him to deliver you. This season will pass, and you will find better days.

# 182 | Known and Cared For

> *You have searched me, LORD, and you know me. You know when I sit and when I rise; you perceive my thoughts from afar.*
>
> **— PSALM 139:1-2**

God knows you better than you know yourself. As the synapses in your brain fire and a thought is formulated, he already knows it. And he still loves you! That's the part that shocks me, I think. Sometimes I find this verse to be an encouragement, while other times it freaks me out. How can he know my thoughts and still want anything to do with me?! Because he's good. Whether God feels close to you or distant, remember you are known and cared for.

# 183 | Compassion for Every Hurt

*I remember my affliction and my wandering, the bitterness and the gall. I well remember them, and my soul is downcast within me. Yet this I call to mind and therefore I have hope: Because of the LORD's great love we are not consumed, for his compassions never fail. They are new every morning; great is your faithfulness.*

**— LAMENTATIONS 3:19–23**

There are many sorrows in this life. Following Jesus won't protect you from them, and it's okay to be real about that. It's no denial of faith to be honest about your business failure, your divorce, your depression, your kids who won't talk to you. Sit in that pain, be honest with it, grieve your losses. And turn your eyes to Jesus, who loves you, weeps with you, and will restore your hope and strength. He is faithful.

## Live Out the Word

Are you the kind of man who glosses over hardships, faking a smile? Why might that be?

Are you the kind of man who gets stuck in despair, unable to move on? What might help you change that?

Counseling, therapy, medicine, healthy food, exercise, laughter, and the presence of loving community are all spiritually valid ways that God renews us. What haven't you tried yet?

# 184 | Contemplative Silence

> *This is what the Sovereign LORD, the Holy One of Israel, says: "In repentance and rest is your salvation, in quietness and trust is your strength."*
>
> **— ISAIAH 30:15A**

Male strength is often loud and flashy, but God invites us to a different kind of strength, one that is quiet and unseen. The practice of spiritual contemplation involves sitting in silence, not praying with words but quelling your thoughts in order to notice God's presence around you. Contemplating his goodness in private will expose areas of your heart and mind that do not trust him, that feel awkward about such intimacy, and that worry this is all a waste of time. That's the point.

# 185 | The Lord's Peace on You

> *"Though the mountains be shaken and the hills be removed, yet my unfailing love for you will not be shaken nor my covenant of peace be removed,"* says the LORD, who has compassion on you.
>
> **— ISAIAH 54:10**

The earthquakes of our lives often cause us to doubt God's presence or his faithful care. When a tree falls on the house and the repairs put us into debt or someone rear-ends us and we end up with chronic pain, it's common to ask why this happened and where God was. God promises that his unfailing love is always with us. Nothing needs to change. You are still in the center of his gaze.

# 186 | Boundless Resources

> *I am the LORD, the God of all mankind.*
> *Is anything too hard for me?*
>
> **— JEREMIAH 32:27**

When my wife and I were renting our first apartment, it was a real stretch to collect the first and last month's rent that was required as a deposit. We had found a great apartment in a good area but worried the finances would fall through. Suddenly, the peace of God washed over me, and I felt him say, "Do you think I would provide the perfect home for you only to forget about the money?" I was humbled, and the funds came in shortly after. Nothing is impossible for God.

# 187 | Mercy, Not Sacrifice

> *For I desire mercy, not sacrifice, and acknowledgment*
> *of God rather than burnt offerings.*
>
> **— HOSEA 6:6**

As a foster parent, I've met children who have endured terrible things. Nothing is quite as heartbreaking as a child who blames themself for their traumatic experiences, determines they are a bad person, and attempts to punish themself. As a pastor, I've seen people do the same with God, believing that the Old Testament demands their self-punishing offerings and sacrifices. But the law of Moses was more of an accommodation of prehistoric ritual violence than a reflection of God's ways. God was never out for blood; he desires mercy—for us and from us.

# 188 | A Glimpse of Things to Come

> *And afterward, I will pour out my Spirit on all people.*
> *Your sons and daughters will prophesy, your old men*
> *will dream dreams, your young men will see visions.*
>
> **– JOEL 2:28**

In ancient times, prophecy and visions were the domain of a select few, such as Joel. If you wanted to hear what God had to say, you had to go find a prophet. Writing at least four hundred years before Jesus was born, Joel caught a glimpse of the coming Holy Spirit and how things would change. The Hebrew word translated "all people" in this verse literally means "the whole of flesh." If you're a human being, God's Spirit is on you.

# 189 | The Good Father

> *I will not leave you as orphans; I will come to you.*
>
> **– JOHN 14:18**

Ideally, fathers protect us, provide for us, and give us identity. If raised with kindness and compassion, us boys are equipped with the strength and courage to grow up and become men who father others well ourselves. That's been a mixed bag for all of us, so it's good to remember that the promise of God's Spirit is also the promise that we would have a Father–not a violent, angry, absent, or deadbeat dad but a present, powerful, good Father who understands us and teaches us well.

# 190 | The Promise Fulfilled

> *They saw what seemed to be tongues of fire that separated and came to rest on each of them. All of them were filled with the Holy Spirit and began to speak in other tongues as the Spirit enabled them.*
>
> **— ACTS 2:3–4**

Jesus had instructed his friends to wait in Jerusalem until the Advocate, the Helper, came to them. When the Holy Spirit did, the results were explosive. Fishermen were transformed into preachers and prophets, and they were given foreign languages to share God's love with everyone. And that was just the beginning! Have you experienced the baptism of the Holy Spirit? If not, welcome the Holy Spirit (who is already present) to make a home in you.

# 191 | Temples Made of Flesh

> *Don't you know that you yourselves are God's temple and that God's Spirit dwells in your midst?*
>
> **— 1 CORINTHIANS 3:16**

Jesus once told his audience that if their temple was torn down, he could rebuild it in three days. The temple had been under construction for forty-six years, so people were outraged. They didn't understand Jesus was talking about his body, the temple of the living God, foreshadowing what would become true for all of us shortly thereafter. You don't need to go to church to find God, though you're allowed to try. You are the temple of God himself. His Spirit is all around you, whether you know it or not.

# 192 | No Matter What

> *For physical training is of some value, but godliness has value for all things, holding promise for both the present life and the life to come.*
>
> **— 1 TIMOTHY 4:8**

I hope you are confident by now that there's nothing we must or can do to please God or earn his favor. We are loved and chosen, no matter what. But the new life that Jesus promised by his Spirit should impact our behavior and the way we take up space in this world. Going to the gym is fine, maybe even fun, but being built up in God's way of love will affect everything and everyone around us.

# 193 | This New Life

> *Religion that God our Father accepts as pure and faultless is this: to look after orphans and widows in their distress and to keep oneself from being polluted by the world.*
>
> **— JAMES 1:27**

Over the next few weeks, we're going to look at the practical implications of following Jesus and having his Spirit dwell within us. I'm not talking about trying hard to be a good Christian. I'm talking about surrendering to the work the Spirit is doing in your life. This is what it looks like when men take up their crosses and follow Jesus: They care about children and elderly women and the condition of their own hearts.

# 194 | Choose Your Investments

*Whoever sows to please their flesh, from the flesh will reap destruction; whoever sows to please the Spirit, from the Spirit will reap eternal life.*

**— GALATIANS 6:8**

Remember that according to John, eternal life is knowing God. You and I are in a process whereby more and more parts of our personhood are coming to know God. As we surrender new areas of ourselves to God, trusting him instead of managing things ourselves, we experience more life and more joy in these areas. If we continue to be driven by our fears or selfishly look out only for ourselves, God doesn't condemn us for that. But we miss out on new ways of living.

# 195 | Canceling Debts

*Be kind and compassionate to one another, forgiving each other, just as in Christ God forgave you.*

**— EPHESIANS 4:32**

To forgive someone is to cancel their debt, to release one who has wronged you from having to make it right. It requires us to trust that God will take care of whatever it is that was genuinely taken from us. Forgiveness doesn't mean you must be friends again, but if you do want to be reconciled, forgiveness is part of that process. A practice that helps me forgive is to picture myself in a great river of forgiveness coming from the heart of God. I let his forgiveness flow through me to others.

# 196 | Grace and Bitterness

> *Make every effort to live in peace with everyone and to be holy; without holiness no one will see the Lord. See to it that no one falls short of the grace of God and that no bitter root grows up to cause trouble and defile many.*
>
> **— HEBREWS 12:14–15**

Either our entire lives and the lives of everyone else are covered by God's grace or nothing is. To avoid bitterness, we must learn to forgive and live at peace with everyone. This is what grace helps us do, and it's what makes us holy (set apart). Can you let God's grace be enough for other people? What about for yourself?

# 197 | Pleasant Conversation

> *Let your conversation be always full of grace, seasoned with salt, so that you may know how to answer everyone.*
>
> **— COLOSSIANS 4:6**

Spending time with people who complain or gossip or bad-mouth others can be exhausting. As we see in Jesus, true generosity of spirit is found in humility and kindness. If you know you're a complainer, then ask the Spirit to help you develop kind and generous speech. Observe your own language and submit yourself to God and others, who will help you become more full of grace. It's useful professionally as well—most people prefer to be around folks whose speech edifies and encourages them.

# 198 | Pray for Others

> *I urge, then, first of all, that petitions, prayers, intercession and thanksgiving be made for all people—for kings and all those in authority, that we may live peaceful and quiet lives in all godliness and holiness.*
>
> **— 1 TIMOTHY 2:1–2**

Jesus regularly took time to pray and so should we. Whether we offer long or short prayers, our own prayers or those written by saints long passed, the point is to bring people and situations before God and lay them at his feet. Prayer is a mystery. No one knows exactly how or why it works, but something dynamic happens when we align ourselves with God's compassion for the world.

# 199 | Becoming Your Brother's Keeper

> *Carry each other's burdens, and in this way you will fulfill the law of Christ.*
>
> **— GALATIANS 6:2**

When Cain killed his brother Abel, God asked him where his brother was. Cain snapped back, "How should I know? Am I my brother's keeper?" The long narrative of scripture, culminating in Jesus carrying the burdens of us all and inviting us to take up our crosses and follow him, seems to answer Cain's question: Yes, we are our brothers' keepers. And who are our brothers? Anyone made in the image of God. Through compassionate presence, prayer, and practical action, we can carry the burdens of those God puts in our path.

## 200 | Integrity of Speech

> *Therefore each of you must put off falsehood and speak truthfully to your neighbor, for we are all members of one body.*
>
> **— EPHESIANS 4:25**

There are various reasons that we tell lies. Typically, it's to preserve our reputations, but it can also be to avoid difficult conversations or to protect others. Whatever the reason, while God never condemns us for our broken behaviors, we are called to a higher standard. Men who follow Jesus should be mindful of their integrity, being true to their word and shunning all falsehood. Note that this includes self-serving exaggeration, which is one of my temptations. Let your heart and your words tell the truth.

## 201 | Reading the Bible

> *From infancy you have known the Holy Scriptures, which are able to make you wise for salvation through faith in Christ Jesus.*
>
> **— 2 TIMOTHY 3:15**

If you read the Introduction, you'll know I've had a complicated relationship with the Bible. I've ignored it for years at a time, frustrated by stories I didn't understand. I've also found it a source of hope and clarity, a lifeline in times of trouble. Two things are true: (1) Reading scripture is a helpful and transformative practice, and (2) we need the Holy Spirit to illuminate it for us. Paul explains to Timothy that the point of scripture is faith in Jesus. That's a good plumb line.

## 202 | Walking in the Light

> *Therefore confess your sins to each other and pray for each other so that you may be healed. The prayer of a righteous person is powerful and effective.*
>
> **– JAMES 5:16**

If you have been a victim of spiritual abuse, then being asked to confess your sins to one another might sound quite triggering. Ideally, with hearts ruled by grace, confession should be a life-giving practice. Bringing your hidden failures into the light by sharing them with trusted brothers in the Lord disarms their power to torment you. Praying for one another with honesty about our needs builds strong bonds of love and trust between us. Do you have such a band of brothers to journey with?

## 203 | Learning to Submit

> *Trust in the LORD with all your heart and lean not on your own understanding; in all your ways submit to him, and he will make your paths straight.*
>
> **– PROVERBS 3:5–6**

Following Jesus means you're not in charge anymore. This is difficult for many of us men, who were raised to be self-sufficient and in charge. It's hard for many women, too. Divine life comes to us through humble submission because the Trinity of God–Father, Son, and Spirit–are mutually submitted to one another. Trust and submission are the currency of divine life. What aspect of this is hardest for you to accept? Why do you think that is?

# 204 | Leaders for a Season

*Remember your leaders, who spoke the word
of God to you. Consider the outcome
of their way of life and imitate their faith.*

**— HEBREWS 13:7**

Some of us have been burned in the past by domineering or controlling leaders, people who devalued our freedom and agency. That kind of leadership is toxic and isn't appropriate for a follower of Jesus. But following Jesus isn't a solo affair. It is meant to be done in beloved community, where natural leaders will emerge for a season. Look around you, find figures of wisdom and maturity, and let them mentor you when you need it. Pray for them and model their faithfulness.

# 205 | Unity through Peace

*Be completely humble and gentle; be patient, bearing
with one another in love. Make every effort to
keep the unity of the Spirit through the bond of peace.*

**— EPHESIANS 4:2-3**

The men Jesus picked to become his disciples, and the women who followed and supported them, came from a wide range of backgrounds. Militant zealots, religious purists, despised tax collectors, fishermen—they were all welcomed by Jesus, but they had to learn to get along. Over three years they were molded into a functional community where their differences were celebrated but didn't result in chaos. We desperately need to learn how to keep the unity of the Spirit today.

# 206 | Continual Transformation

*Do not conform to the pattern of this world, but be transformed by the renewing of your mind. Then you will be able to test and approve what God's will is—his good, pleasing and perfect will.*

**— ROMANS 12:2**

I've been married for over fifteen years, and I keep learning more about who my wife is and how to love her. Being transformed by Jesus is the same: There may have been a moment when you chose to turn toward him, but growing in love and divine life is an ongoing process. Time spent in community, in silent contemplation and prayer, reading scripture, and serving others all help form Jesus in us.

# 207 | Lift Up Your Eyes

*Since, then, you have been raised with Christ, set your hearts on things above, where Christ is, seated at the right hand of God.*

**— COLOSSIANS 3:1**

There are 101 things that demand our attention. Providing for our family, serving our community, rest, and entertainment when we need it, but also destructive things like workaholism, obsession with wealth, and pointless arguments. We should be diligent in directing our attention to God, listening to his voice, and letting him guide our focus and attention. If we're not intentional, our energy will be sucked toward whatever distracting centers of gravity our culture offers.

# 208 | Sexual Sanctity

> *It is God's will that you should be sanctified: that*
> *you should avoid sexual immorality; that each of you*
> *should learn to control your own body in a way*
> *that is holy and honorable, not in passionate lust like*
> *the pagans, who do not know God.*
>
> **— 1 THESSALONIANS 4:3–5**

Let's be clear: God values sexual pleasure. He invented your penis and knows how it works. He gave women a clitoris, the sole purpose of which is to provide pleasure. Sex is meant to be enjoyed! But it was meant to be enjoyed intentionally, within the bond of mutual love. Anything that you and your partner do not agree is life-giving or pleasing to God is off-limits to you both. Everything else, go wild!

# 209 | Your Mouth Is a Mirror

> *Those who consider themselves religious and*
> *yet do not keep a tight rein on their tongues deceive*
> *themselves, and their religion is worthless.*
>
> **— JAMES 1:26**

Some people attend church and read their Bible but don't actually follow the way of Jesus wholeheartedly. James, the half-brother of Jesus, was particularly concerned about this. Inappropriate things might include lying, gossip, slander, complaining, or just hours of idle, pointless chatter. We are invited to be intentional about our speech so that our whole body reflects God's goodness and declares his presence.

## 210 | Youthful Witnesses

> *Don't let anyone look down on you because you are young, but set an example for the believers in speech, in conduct, in love, in faith and in purity.*
>
> **— 1 TIMOTHY 4:12**

Jesus was in his early thirties when he preached. Timothy, Paul's protégé, was probably even younger. We've already talked about Mary, who was younger still. Age is no qualifier for righteousness or faithfulness. If you have become a mentor or leader to others, don't let anyone's resentment of your age hold you back from setting a good example. Be steadfast, and in time, the older folks who judge you now might just be humbled by your faithfulness.

## 211 | A Life of Prayer

> *But you, dear friends, by building yourselves up in your most holy faith and praying in the Holy Spirit, keep yourselves in God's love as you wait for the mercy of our Lord Jesus Christ to bring you to eternal life.*
>
> **— JUDE 1:20–21**

One of the ways we are built up and brought toward the knowledge of God is prayer. Time spent lifting up others before God grows compassion and faithfulness in us. There is no set rule or requirement you must follow, but developing a structured discipline of prayer has been helpful for many across the centuries. Add five minutes of prayer to your morning routine and see what happens after a month.

# 212 | Stewarding God's Children

*Fathers, do not exasperate your children; instead, bring them up in the training and instruction of the Lord.*

**— EPHESIANS 6:4**

I know some men who were exasperated by their fathers. Constantly nitpicking, belittling kids over failures or mistakes, and pushing them too hard to succeed are all recipes for exasperation. This is not the way our Father treats us. If you're a dad, be patient with your kids, help them see the things they don't see, and trust the Holy Spirit to be at work in their lives just as it is in yours. They were God's children before they were yours, so tread lightly.

# 213 | Stay Free

*It is for freedom that Christ has set us free. Stand firm, then, and do not let yourselves be burdened again by a yoke of slavery.*

**— GALATIANS 5:1**

Many religious people are enslaved to rules they think God has put on them. They toil hard for a master rather than enjoy the presence of a Father who loves them and the freedom he gives. Jesus came to set us free from this kind of bondage, too. As a follower of Jesus, you are free to live however the Spirit leads you. If your freedom might provoke those who are less free, don't let their judgment get under your skin. Stay free.

# 214 | Laying Down Your Life

> *I eagerly expect and hope that I will in no way be ashamed, but will have sufficient courage so that now as always Christ will be exalted in my body, whether by life or by death.*
>
> **— PHILIPPIANS 1:20**

The earliest followers of Jesus were united in their expectation of dying for their faith. So embodied was their conviction that political leaders felt threatened enough to have them killed. Church tradition tells us that Paul and all but one of Jesus's disciples were executed. That should give us pause before we complain about our rights and freedoms.

# 215 | Wholeness of Heart

> *Teach me your way, LORD, that I may rely on your faithfulness; give me an undivided heart, that I may fear your name.*
>
> **— PSALM 86:11**

The painful things that happen to us in life can leave traumatic scars that impact the way we conduct ourselves. Turning to follow Jesus doesn't immediately heal all our trauma or change deeply ingrained behaviors. Followers of Jesus should excavate their hearts to find places resistant to the Holy Spirit's work. Through good professional therapy and the healing power of the Spirit, these areas of scar tissue can be softened and healed. It requires great courage to look inward, but God can be found there.

# 216 | A Peaceful Community

*If it is possible, as far as it depends on you,*
*live at peace with everyone.*

**— ROMANS 12:18**

This one always feels like a tall order. Live at peace with everyone? It can be hard enough just to live at peace with myself, let alone my wife and kids or the people at church who give me a hard time. All things are possible with God, and he doesn't ask more of us than we can give. To live at peace, we must refuse to control others, surrender the outcomes of our interactions, and have good boundaries for our own integrity. Building peaceful community takes time and effort.

# 217 | Thankfulness as a Way of Life

*Rejoice always, pray continually, give*
*thanks in all circumstances; for this is God's*
*will for you in Christ Jesus.*

**— 1 THESSALONIANS 5:16–18**

When we learn to be present in the moment and discern that God is with us, the trials of our present circumstances become much more tolerable. We don't have to like everything about our lives to adopt a posture of joyous trust in God. This too shall pass, and tomorrow will be a new day; we might as well be cheerful until it comes. Giving thanks also helps reframe our perspective and open our eyes to the blessings that pessimism blinds us to.

## 218 | Love Conquers All

> *Therefore, as God's chosen people, holy and dearly loved, clothe yourselves with compassion, kindness, humility, gentleness and patience.*
>
> **— COLOSSIANS 3:12**

What would the world look like if more men were defined by compassion, kindness, humility, gentleness, and patience? I think it would be a remarkable place. That's what the kingdom of heaven is already like, and Jesus promised that his kingdom was at hand, breaking into this world. The more we lean into Jesus, surrendering our willpower to his, the more we will manifest these traits in our own lives. Love conquers all, which makes these traits the truest picture of strength, power, and manliness.

## 219 | Never Too Wise to Learn

> *Let the wise listen and add to their learning, and let the discerning get guidance.*
>
> **— PROVERBS 1:5**

Each one of us is a unique creation staring up at a limitless God. Distinct aspects of his character stand out to each of us, which means it's important to listen to and learn from others. None of us can see the full picture. The journey that God has you on is different from mine, but we can each glean things from what God has revealed to the other. You can never be too wise to learn. In fact, a mark of wisdom is a commitment to lifelong learning and growth.

## 220 | Honor Your Leaders

> *Now we ask you, brothers and sisters, to acknowledge those who work hard among you, who care for you in the Lord and who admonish you.*
>
> **— 1 THESSALONIANS 5:12**

In most communities, 20 percent of the people do 80 percent of the work, whether they are appointed leaders or not. There are many reasons for this, and it's not an indictment on those doing less work. Some are resting for a season, some are receiving here while serving elsewhere, and others are new and have yet to find the place where their gifts fit best. In any case, honor those who work hard to serve your community, whatever their roles are.

## 221 | A Team of Leaders

> *And the things you have heard me say in the presence of many witnesses entrust to reliable people who will also be qualified to teach others.*
>
> **— 2 TIMOTHY 2:2**

The first decade of my career was in charity management, and before I learned to staff both my weaknesses and my strengths, I had become an indispensable, overachieving bottleneck. This felt flattering but burned me out and didn't equip others to lead. The apostle Paul wrote many words of pastoral care to Timothy. Here he focused on the need to find reliable people who could faithfully pass on his teachings to others, ensuring that Timothy wouldn't become a bottleneck.

# 222 | What the Spirit Does in Us

> *But the fruit of the Spirit is love, joy, peace, forbearance, kindness, goodness, faithfulness, gentleness and self-control. Against such things there is no law.*
>
> **— GALATIANS 5:22-23**

Ask the average person on the street to describe a Christian, and you might hear things like judgmental, homophobic, naive, closed-minded, deluded, superstitious, and so on. This is a tragic indictment about those who are meant to radiate the best kind of love. It would seem that many who wear the label "Christian" have not actually allowed the Spirit to produce much fruit in their lives. May the future be filled with men and women whose lives overflow with love, joy, peace, patience, kindness, goodness, faithfulness, gentleness, and self-control. The world needs more of them.

## Live Out the Word

What does the fruit of your life look like? Would people describe you as modeling the traits listed in today's verse?

What traits do you notice are commonplace but are missing from this list (e.g., divisive, quickly angered, easily offended)?

Which one of these fruits is the most absent from your life? Over the next ten days, pray daily for the Spirit to increase this in you.

## 223 | Where Moth and Rust Destroy . . .

> *Command those who are rich in this present world not to be arrogant nor to put their hope in wealth, which is so uncertain, but to put their hope in God, who richly provides us with everything for our enjoyment.*
>
> **— 1 TIMOTHY 6:17**

There is nothing inherently wrong with material wealth, but the writers of the New Testament have many strong words for the rich. It seems exceptionally difficult for those with great material wealth to maintain true humility and not conflate their affluence with power, authority, and God's blessing. Money comes and money goes, but God remains steadfast. The indwelling life of Jesus is your best investment for now and for eternity.

## 224 | Enough for Today

> *Keep your lives free from the love of money and be content with what you have, because God has said, "Never will I leave you; never will I forsake you."*
>
> **— HEBREWS 13:5**

A bigger house, a better car, new clothes, fun toys, the latest phone–the list of things the world offers to make us happier and feel cooler is endless. The way of Jesus is to live simply and be content with what you have. That doesn't mean you can't buy the things you need to serve your family well–you should. But don't pursue or rely on wealth to make you happy. Let the presence of God satisfy your soul.

## 225 | Feel Satisfied

*Each one should test their own actions. Then they can take pride in themselves alone, without comparing themselves to someone else, for each one should carry their own load.*

**— GALATIANS 6:4-5**

Comparing ourselves to others has always been a trap, but social media has turned it into an art form. So many of us share content that looks authentic but is actually all curated, while the filtered lives of others make us feel insufficient. What God invites you to carry is unique. At the end of today, feel satisfied in what you and God have done together.

## 226 | Posture Yourself for Peace

*Do not be anxious about anything, but in every situation, by prayer and petition, with thanksgiving, present your requests to God. And the peace of God, which transcends all understanding, will guard your hearts and your minds in Christ Jesus.*

**— PHILIPPIANS 4:6-7**

If you have an anxiety disorder, rest assured the apostle Paul isn't calling you out. He's addressing those who worry endlessly and don't turn to God with their fears and frustrations. This passage is a good reminder—for all of us—that an intentional posture of trust and thankfulness is the best way toward a peace that surpasses the logic of our circumstances.

# 227 | Honor Is Freely Given

> *In the same way, you who are younger, submit yourselves to your elders. All of you, clothe yourselves with humility toward one another, because, "God opposes the proud but shows favor to the humble."*
>
> **— 1 PETER 5:5**

It took me until my thirties to really appreciate the wisdom of my elders. In my teens, I had known so many older folks who demanded my obedience and respect without any humility of their own. But humility and honor only work as gifts freely given. Find a mentor you respect and learn from them.

# 228 | A Better Way

> *Bear with each other and forgive one another if any of you has a grievance against someone. Forgive as the Lord forgave you.*
>
> **— COLOSSIANS 3:13**

Even in the beloved community of Jesus followers, we end up hurting one another. It is important that we repent, that we admit our shortcomings to our brothers and sisters, forgive one another for our failings, and do not hold grudges. Toxic abusers must be dealt with differently, but each of us must still do our part to forgive; otherwise, we remain in bondage. The world is watching the way we love, and we seem pretty bad at it right now. I have hope that Jesus will lead us to a better way.

# 229 | Poverty Is Unjust

> *If anyone has material possessions and sees a brother or sister in need but has no pity on them, how can the love of God be in that person?*
>
> **— 1 JOHN 3:17**

The early followers of Jesus saw the poverty around them as a sign of injustice, an outcome of exploitation and greed. Neo-liberal, free market capitalism has trained us to see poor people as lazy and not doing enough for themselves. But most people throughout history have been poor! To be comfortably housed and well fed is extremely rare. Our modern comforts are a gracious blessing, and most of us have more than enough to share with those in need.

# 230 | Dishonesty Is Complicated

> *Do not lie to each other, since you have taken off your old self with its practices.*
>
> **— COLOSSIANS 3:9**

The writers of the New Testament really seem concerned about lying and dishonesty. When we lie to others, we impact their ability to trust us, and we reduce the amount of integrity present in our relationships. Lies have a way of being exposed, which either requires us to fess up or to lie again. Dishonesty is a very complicated way of life. In Jesus, we are invited to radical honesty precisely because we are loved and never condemned. There's really no need to lie.

# 231 | Serve in Love

> *You, my brothers and sisters, were called to be free.*
> *But do not use your freedom to indulge*
> *the flesh; rather, serve one another humbly in love.*

## — GALATIANS 5:13

Paul is not complaining about our physical bodies. Indulging the flesh has little to do with our atoms and cells; it's a reference to anything that opposes our surrender to the Holy Spirit. Jesus has given us all freedom, but some of the things we are "free" to do are not harmonious with his life inside us. You cannot serve others humbly in love by abusing, manipulating, lying, or stealing.

# 232 | A Simple Life

> *Make it your ambition to lead a quiet life: You should*
> *mind your own business and work with your*
> *hands, just as we told you, so that your daily life may*
> *win the respect of outsiders and so*
> *that you will not be dependent on anybody.*

## — 1 THESSALONIANS 4:11–12

I grew up with two different lives: one surrounded by cows, cornfields, and sheep and the other living in big cities, a child of missionaries preaching the gospel. I spent much of the first thirty years of my life trying to change the world. Now, it seems that living a simple life, following Jesus, and caring for those around us is all we were ever called to do.

## 233 | Living Sacrifices

> *Therefore, I urge you, brothers and sisters, in view*
> *of God's mercy, to offer your bodies*
> *as a living sacrifice, holy and pleasing to God—*
> *this is your true and proper worship.*
>
> **— ROMANS 12:1**

This call to be living sacrifices could be thought of as a summation of all Paul's letters. God has ended ritual sacrifice and set us free from all bondage, including the fear of punishment and death. He has written his love upon our hearts forever. We are free to follow Jesus into lives of joyful mission, relishing his love and displaying for everyone around us just how good God is. A living sacrifice is a life of others-centered, co-suffering love.

## 234 | Oriented toward Goodness

> *Finally, brothers and sisters, whatever is true, whatever*
> *is noble, whatever is right, whatever is pure, whatever*
> *is lovely, whatever is admirable—if anything is excellent*
> *or praiseworthy—think about such things.*
>
> **— PHILIPPIANS 4:8**

Jesus also went to parties, hung out with his friends, prayed, and rested. His life was oriented toward goodness and compassion in all its forms, and ours should be as well. I'm not saying a follower of Jesus can't watch *Game of Thrones* (I happen to enjoy plenty of HBO), but let's ensure that our attention is primarily focused on good, life-giving things.

# 235 | The Tenacity of the Saints

> *For everything that was written in the past*
> *was written to teach us, so that through the endurance*
> *taught in the Scriptures and the*
> *encouragement they provide we might have hope.*
>
> **— ROMANS 15:4**

Closing out this section of practical teaching, where do we find hope and encouragement? In stories of endurance. Paul, writing to his friends in Rome, didn't know that his letters would one day be considered scripture. All this Jesus-following Jewish man knew is the stories of God's faithfulness to his ancestors and their endurance in the face of seemingly endless trials. And that's his prayer of blessing: May the tenacity of the saints long passed give you hope.

# 236 | To the Victor Go the Spoils

> *To the one who is victorious, I will give the right*
> *to sit with me on my throne, just as I was victorious*
> *and sat down with my Father on his throne.*
>
> **— REVELATION 3:21**

These words of Jesus used to freak me out a little, as if his blessing would be withheld if I didn't do a good job. Today, though, I think it's just an honest assessment of reality. If we are faithful to the way of Jesus, loving others and overcoming temptation by his Spirit within us, we will enjoy the knowledge that we did. And if we don't, then we are caught in the hands of grace nonetheless.

## 237 | You're Amazing

> *I praise you because I am fearfully and wonderfully made; your works are wonderful, I know that full well.*
>
> **— PSALM 139:14**

Let me paraphrase this one for you: "You can thank and honor God, because he did an excellent job making you. Everything he makes is awesome, including you, and you're allowed to agree with that." Are you comfortable praising God because of your own awesomeness? The psalmist seems to have been. While our culture presents options for both outrageous self-aggrandizement and devastating self-deprecation, God invites us to love ourselves with humble honesty. He made us, and he only makes good things. Including you.

## 238 | A Mighty River

> *But let justice roll on like a river, righteousness like a never-failing stream!*
>
> **— AMOS 5:24**

One day Jesus will return to judge the living and the dead. When the one who is love itself comes to judge the world, he will set all things right. If you've been oppressed because of your race, your height, your sexuality, or the way your brain works, if you've never been able to provide for your family the way you wanted to, if you've felt the sting of injustice for any reason, then let this prayer be your prayer. Let justice and righteousness flow like a mighty river!

# 239 | Resurrection Life

*For if we have been united with him in a death
like his, we will certainly also be
united with him in a resurrection like his.*

**— ROMANS 6:5**

When Jesus died, all humanity died with him, and when the
Father raised Jesus from the dead, all humanity came, too.
When your old sources of shame and temptation come
knocking, you can let Jesus answer the door and tell them
the news: You don't live here anymore, you died. Of course,
you didn't stay that way. Like Jesus, new life runs through
your veins, and this new life is very good.

# 240 | Saintly Sisters

*Now Deborah, a prophet, the wife of Lappidoth,
was leading Israel at that time.*

**— JUDGES 4:4**

A faithful reading of biblical and Christian tradition reveals
many female leaders, teachers, pastors, and evangelists.
Many of the faith lessons in my life were taught by women,
especially my mother, my grandmothers, and countless
preachers, prophets, and theologians. While both church
and college have often precluded women from formal training or ministry roles, they have been doing the work anyway,
faithfully serving God and family for generations. Are you a
man who promotes women?

# 241 | Dark Forces

> *For our struggle is not against flesh and blood, but against the rulers, against the authorities, against the powers of this dark world and against the spiritual forces of evil in the heavenly realms.*
>
> **— EPHESIANS 6:12**

No human is truly your enemy. Every person who hurts you, any government or corporation that exploits its power is unwittingly serving the agenda of unseen spiritual powers. These dark forces have already been defeated by Jesus on the cross, but they cause havoc anywhere humans move against the way of love. Prayer and faithful witness are their undoing.

# 242 | Strategy of Love

> *His intent was that now, through the church, the manifold wisdom of God should be made known to the rulers and authorities in the heavenly realms.*
>
> **— EPHESIANS 3:10**

Although the systems and powers that oppose God's good work in this world are real, we don't fight them by waving crosses or throwing holy water. God will eventually make all things right, and his solution for the time being is the unity of the church. When the beloved community of Jesus faithfully models others-centered, co-suffering love to those around them, the spiritual powers are shamed, and their influence is diminished.

> *The body is not made up of one part but of many.... If the whole body were an eye, where would the sense of hearing be? If the whole body were an ear, where would the sense of smell be? But in fact, God has placed the parts in the body, every one of them, just as he wanted them to be.... If one part suffers, every part suffers with it; if one part is honored, every part rejoices with it. Now you are the body of Christ, and each one of you is a part of it.*
>
> **— 1 CORINTHIANS 12:14, 17-18, 26-27**

Paul often uses the metaphor of a body to describe the diversity and unity that God intends for the global community of Jesus followers. Every person is different and unique and welcome. The same applies to races, tribes, denominations, and any other kind of grouping. We all have something to contribute to the whole, and no one is less worthy or valuable than another. The body is diminished when any one part is rejected.

## Live Out the Word

Are your gifts seen and valued by your community? What could improve this?

What kinds of people would you honestly prefer weren't in the body at all? Why is that?

What steps could you take to reframe your perspective and see them as valuable?

What kinds of people are devalued in your community right now? What can you do about this?

# 244 | Head, Shoulders, Knees, and Toes

> *And he is the head of the body, the church; he is the*
> *beginning and the firstborn from among the dead, so*
> *that in everything he might have the supremacy.*
> *For God was pleased to have all his fullness dwell in him.*
>
> **— COLOSSIANS 1:18–19**

If the followers of Jesus make up a body, then Jesus alone is its head. Much like the way that your body responds to your brain's control and guidance, we are to be led by Jesus, who sees and hears all. If he were a harsh ruler, this would be a real cause for concern, but he is pure life and light and love. All of who God is dwells in Jesus, and Jesus is but the first of this new species we are becoming.

# 245 | No-Revenge Mindsets

> *You should not gloat over your brother in the day*
> *of his misfortune, nor rejoice over the people*
> *of Judah in the day of their destruction, nor boast*
> *so much in the day of their trouble.*
>
> **— OBADIAH 1:12**

When someone who has opposed us comes to harm, it's tempting to feel a measure of satisfaction. When people get what is coming to them, it seems like there may be some justice in the universe after all. But this attitude comes from a mindset of punishment and revenge, not love for enemies and restoration of all that is broken. Resist this way of thinking and submit yourself to the Spirit for transformation.

## 246 | Extravagance vs. Stoicism

> *How priceless is your unfailing love, O God!*
> *People take refuge in the shadow of your wings.*
> *They feast on the abundance of your house;*
> *you give them drink from your river of delights.*
>
> **— PSALM 36:7–8**

If your image of God still leans toward a masculine figure that is cool, reserved, and stoic, try this on for size: God is a bird, and you can safely hide under his wings. God keeps the pantry full of delicious food. God dips a ladle into a river of wine to pour you a glass. This is all poetic language to help us see that God is nothing short of extravagant in his love for us.

## 247 | Continuously Unfolding Revelation

> *Those who think they know something do not*
> *yet know as they ought to know.*
> *But whoever loves God is known by God.*
>
> **— 1 CORINTHIANS 8:2–3**

I once led the kids at our church in a journaling exercise and instructed them to ask God to reveal something unique or surprising to them about himself via words or a picture. I did the exercise too and felt the Spirit say to me quite clearly, "You have no idea who I am." Touché. When we think we have God figured out, we're only just getting started. We should all leave plenty of room for ourselves to keep learning as we go.

# 248 | Fearless Grace

> *So do not fear, for I am with you; do not be dismayed,*
> *for I am your God. I will strengthen you and help you;*
> *I will uphold you with my righteous right hand.*
>
> **— ISAIAH 41:10**

Eventually you and I are just going to have to accept that we have nothing to fear, not from this life and not from God. Every time you fall short of the mark and cover yourself in condemnation, God wipes the grime off you. Whenever your enemies seem to surround you, God reaches down and lifts you up to a higher place. It may not make a lot of sense, but God is with us, and God is good.

# 249 | A Righteous Judge . . . Doesn't Judge

> *Moreover, the Father judges no one, but has*
> *entrusted all judgment to the Son. . . . You judge by*
> *human standards; I pass judgment on no one.*
>
> **— JOHN 5:22; 8:15**

The Jesus described in John's gospel seems relentless in his refusal to judge or condemn anyone. All who come receive grace and mercy; even simple corrective instruction is rare. Yet people walk away healed and empowered to live whole lives. In my observation, whole people do much less damage to themselves and the world around them. Is it really that simple? Do condemnation and guilt produce nothing of value at all?

# 250 | Holy Memory

*The LORD is my light and my salvation—*
*whom shall I fear? The LORD is the stronghold of*
*my life—of whom shall I be afraid?*

**— PSALM 27:1**

One of the most helpful and long-lasting ways to use scrip-ture is to memorize it. This passage, sung as a hymn, was etched into my memory at a young age. It often comes to mind during times of trial and of boredom, each of which require their own kind of courage. The Psalms are especially good for memorization, though Jewish boys were trained to memorize the entire Torah and more. Try memorizing this passage and come back to it throughout the day.

# 251 | To Stand, Fall

*Even youths grow tired and weary, and*
*young men stumble and fall; but those who hope*
*in the LORD will renew their strength.*

**— ISAIAH 40:30–31A**

What stands out to me today as I dwell on this passage is that God doesn't always prevent us from stumbling. That is not to say that he doesn't care about our scraped knees and stubbed toes, but that stumbling is no great offense to him. Even strong, strapping young men stumble and fall sometimes. That's just a fact. Equally true is that anyone who hopes in God will find their strength renewed, empow-ering them to stand up once again.

## 252 | The Outcome of God

> *For the word of God is alive and active. Sharper than any double-edged sword, it penetrates even to dividing soul and spirit, joints and marrow; it judges the thoughts and attitudes of the heart. Nothing in all creation is hidden from God's sight.*
>
> **— HEBREWS 4:12–13A**

This "word" of God is *logos*, a Greek term that can refer to words, logic, an organizing force, or the outcome of a decision (and much more). As in John 1:1, it's obvious that the writer of Hebrews means far more than the sound of holy lips or the text on holy pages. This "word" is the embodied expression of all that God wants and is. We call him Jesus, and nothing is hidden from him.

## 253 | Imprinted on the Heart

> *Sacrifice and offering you did not desire—but my ears you have opened—burnt offerings and sin offerings you did not require. Then I said, "Here I am, I have come —it is written about me in the scroll. I desire to do your will, my God; your law is within my heart."*
>
> **— PSALM 40:6–8**

This psalm is attributed to King David, and it is another excellent choice for memorization. A close read reveals it as a breathtaking prophecy of the Messiah, who would be David's own descendant, Jesus. The Son of God would carry the law within his heart, imprint it on ours, take away sacrifice, and give us the gift of obedience.

## 254 | Coming Home to Love

*For God did not appoint us to suffer wrath but to receive
salvation through our Lord Jesus Christ.*

**— 1 THESSALONIANS 5:9**

The wrath of God has been used as an evangelistic scare
tactic for generations. I know countless followers of Jesus
who struggle to accept that the Father loves them because
they were frightened into faith in the first place. Fear might
be effective in the short term, but any relationship built on
it is toxic by nature. People stay in abusive relationships
for many reasons, especially because it's what they know.
You're allowed to leave and be welcomed home by the
Father of love.

## 255 | Tenacious Promises

*I remain confident of this: I will see the goodness
of the LORD in the land of the living.*

**— PSALM 27:13**

Another powerful way to use scripture is as a declaration.
We do this by speaking out the promises of scripture that
we need to believe and see manifested. I'm not suggest-
ing we ignore our reality and bury our heads in the sand of
scripture but rather that we lay claim to ancient promises
with modern tenacity. Try saying it out loud with me and
repeat it as needed: "I am confident that I will see the goodness of the Lord in the land of the living." Amen.

# 256 | Families of Peace

> *Their children will be mighty in the land; the*
> *generation of the upright will be blessed.*
>
> **— PSALM 112:2**

Here's another declaration to hold on to, especially if you're a father or grandfather. I long for my children to grow up into kind, compassionate, courageous adults. Thankfully, they appear to be well on their way. Each day I'm shocked and puzzled about how much further into adulthood they are. Say it with me out loud: "My children have and will have strength of character. They will help heal this land. They will walk in grace and peace." Repeat as necessary.

# 257 | The Litmus Test of Love

> *Dear friends, let us love one another, for love comes*
> *from God. Everyone who loves has been*
> *born of God and knows God. Whoever does not love*
> *does not know God, because God is love.*
>
> **— 1 JOHN 4:7–8**

This is one of my favorite passages, and in it, John makes at least two mind-blowing suggestions. First, if others-centered, co-suffering love can't be observed in your life, then you don't actually know God—whether you profess to be a Christian or not. Second, if love of others is present in your life, then you are a new creation and you know God—whether you think you do or not. Love upends everything we thought we knew.

## 258 | The End of Control

> *Now the Lord is the Spirit, and where the Spirit*
> *of the Lord is, there is freedom.*
>
> **— 2 CORINTHIANS 3:17**

The Spirit hovers over the face of the earth. We can't go anywhere to escape him. Our very bodies are temples of God's Spirit. This Holy Spirit is the same spirit that animated Jesus, who is the Son of God and the fullness of the revelation of what the Father is like. Since the substance and nature of God is love, freedom and love go hand in hand. That means there's no room in love for control. A follower of Jesus cannot control others or be controlled by anyone.

## 259 | No Longer Enslaved

> *For you did not receive a spirit of slavery to fall back into*
> *fear, but you have received a spirit of adoption. When we*
> *cry, "Abba! Father!" it is that very Spirit bearing witness*
> *with our spirit that we are children of God.*
>
> **— ROMANS 8:15–16 (NRSV)**

The term *chattel slavery* describes when you, your body, and even your offspring are treated as someone's property. If you got free, you would start from nothing; chattel slavery is the ultimate form of control and an attempt to completely dehumanize a person. The opposite is sonship, where you start with everything, including freedom over your body and full access to the family resources. God has declared we are all his children. We are beloved family, not property.

## 260 | Transformative Gentleness

> *Let your gentleness be evident to all. The Lord is near.*
>
> **— PHILIPPIANS 4:5**

The stereotypical frat boy hazing his peers and hassling women is not acting in freedom or strength; he is acting out of bondage to the expectations of childish men. Because freedom and love are so intertwined, when we act against the way of love, we reduce the freedom of others and reveal our own bondage. A son of God can be comfortable in strength and gentleness, passion and peace, kindness and compassion. The Lord is near, and his gentleness changes us. May the Spirit manifest transformative gentleness in you as well.

## 261 | Timing Matters

> *If anyone loudly blesses their neighbor early in the morning, it will be taken as a curse.*
>
> **— PROVERBS 27:14**

When I began writing this devotional, I asked some friends for their favorite passages of scripture. I couldn't tell if this one was sent to me as a gag or seriously, but it works either way. The right sort of thing done at the wrong time is actually the wrong thing. This lack of discernment about timing tends to happen when we're more concerned about ourselves–appearing helpful, proving our point, protecting our reputation–than we are about the other person. Since love is others-centered rather than self-centered, timing matters.

# 262 | Let Me Show You

*For I am the LORD your God who takes hold of your right hand and says to you, Do not fear; I will help you.*

**— ISAIAH 41:13**

One of the big problems with punishment is that it doesn't help or equip anyone to make lasting changes in their life. Punishment tends to promote sneakiness born of pain avoidance more than it does transformation born of a contrite heart. Like a good and loving Father, God helps, teaches, trains, and equips us. He takes hold of our hand and shows us the way we should go. We can model our parenting, our coaching, and our business leading on this approach as well.

# 263 | Agents of Reconciliation

*All this is from God, who reconciled us to himself through Christ and gave us the ministry of reconciliation: that God was reconciling the world to himself in Christ, not counting people's sins against them.*

**— 2 CORINTHIANS 5:18–19A**

I used to think the Father was an angry old man and Jesus was the cool older brother who kept us safe when Dad went on a bender. But this isn't true at all. Jesus only ever acted out the will of the Father, which means God was actively working to reconcile the entire human race to himself, through himself. Now we're invited to become agents of reconciliation, finding those lost children who are ready to turn toward home and pointing out the way.

# 264 | Contagious Community

> *May the God who gives endurance and*
> *encouragement give you the same attitude of mind*
> *toward each other that Christ Jesus had.*
>
> **— ROMANS 15:5**

Jesus and the Twelve who followed him along with his wider group of friends and supporters formed a band of brothers (and sisters!) who did life together. Across endless miles on foot, on waters calm and stormy, in times of hunger and feast, through cold nights and warm days, they built friendships that lasted for decades and changed the world. This beloved community was contagious because of their love for one another. I hope and pray you find this, too.

# 265 | A Desert Oasis

> *The LORD will guide you always; he will satisfy your*
> *needs in a sun-scorched land and will strengthen*
> *your frame. You will be like a well-watered garden,*
> *like a spring whose waters never fail.*
>
> **— ISAIAH 58:11**

The language of this passage recalls the visceral contrasts in a natural landscape. Can you imagine the skin on your face being pulled tight by the sun, your lips parched and cracking? What do you need in a sun-scorched land? Shade? Shelter? A refreshing spring? This is what God provides: fresh, cool water from hidden underground springs to nurture his precious garden, which is you, by the way. You're the garden.

> *We know that the whole creation has been groaning as in the pains of childbirth right up to the present time. Not only so, but we ourselves, who have the firstfruits of the Spirit, groan inwardly as we wait eagerly for our adoption to sonship, the redemption of our bodies.*
>
> **— ROMANS 8:22–23**

There is something present in the fibers of creation that longs for God's sons and daughters to live in the fullness of divine life. Until those made in the image of God take up their mantle and act like God, creation (and everyone in it) groans in anticipation. Does it excite you to think that the cosmos wants you to live like Jesus?

# 267 | Come Quickly!

> *Do not withhold your mercy from me, LORD; may your love and faithfulness always protect me. For troubles without number surround me; my sins have overtaken me, and I cannot see. They are more than the hairs of my head, and my heart fails within me. Be pleased to save me, LORD; come quickly, LORD, to help me.*
>
> **— PSALM 40:11–13**

Here is another beautiful section of Psalm 40 ripe for memorizing and reciting in times of hardship and failure. Or perhaps you've never felt surrounded by troubles? Don't worry, give it time. The realities of the Jesus life have a way of sneaking up on you. Thankfully, we know God is always pleased to help us.

# 268 | The Seeds of Redemption

> *And we know that in all things God works*
> *for the good of those who love him,*
> *who have been called according to his purpose.*
>
> **— ROMANS 8:28**

God's intellect and love are so far beyond our capacities that without ever orchestrating any bad thing in our life, he ensures that all bad things contain the seeds of redemption. Oh, how tough this is to wrap our heads and hearts around. While we weep and shake and beg to know why, God is already rolling up his sleeves to heal us and weave a beautiful tapestry out of the painful detours this broken world inflicts upon us all. You can trust his redemption skills.

# 269 | The Easter Experience

> *But in keeping with his promise we are*
> *looking forward to a new heaven and a new*
> *earth, where righteousness dwells.*
>
> **— 2 PETER 3:13**

The eternal future of the human race is not puffy white clouds and togas. If that's what you've been holding out for, then I'm sorry to burst your bubble, but it's a modern invention. The earliest Jesus followers believed that God would return one day to heal the entire cosmos and resurrect everyone, just like Jesus at Easter. This new earth will be populated by a transformed humanity, and it will be filled with righteousness. It's been a long time coming, but let's keep spreading the word.

# 270 | Sacred Intimacy

> *But whoever is united with the Lord*
> *is one with him in spirit.*
>
> **— 1 CORINTHIANS 6:17**

When a couple gets married, we often talk about them being joined together and becoming one flesh. This relates to intimacy and often has a sexual connotation, but it's also practical–over time, married partners learn each other's secrets and can sometimes finish each other's sentences. God longs to share his secrets with us and carry our burdens, to become an intimate, trusted partner. Because his Spirit dwells within us, we can be intimate with God in a way that's deeper than sexual chemistry. Is that a strange thought?

# 271 | A Gracious Order of Peace

> *Even in darkness light dawns for the upright, for those*
> *who are gracious and compassionate and righteous.*
> *Good will come to those who are generous and lend*
> *freely, who conduct their affairs with justice.*
>
> **— PSALM 112:4–5**

This is a good promise. Life will always have hard times, but it can also be filled with joy and righteousness. The psalmist looks up from the midst of his darkness to God, the source of light, illumination, and hope, and finds graceful divine presence, never withheld. He sees an order to all things, where ultimately those who live just, honest lives will be blessed. Don't grow weary of doing good or being honest. Your reward will come.

> *Therefore put on the full armor of God, so that when the day of evil comes, you may be able to stand your ground, and after you have done everything, to stand. Stand firm then, with the belt of truth buckled around your waist, with the breastplate of righteousness in place, and with your feet fitted with the readiness that comes from the gospel of peace. In addition to all this, take up the shield of faith, with which you can extinguish all the flaming arrows of the evil one. Take the helmet of salvation and the sword of the Spirit, which is the word of God.*
>
> **— EPHESIANS 6:13–17**

All of God's gifts can be used to resist temptation and trial. The truth of his presence, the righteousness we have in Christ, the peace he left with us, our faith in his promise of salvation, and our confidence in everything he has said about us are mighty and effective. When the voice of shame and accusation sounds in your head, remind yourself of all God has given you and stand firm.

## Live Out the Word

Count how many times the scripture passage says "stand." Why do you think this is important?

Which piece of armor chafes you the most? Ask God for a fresh revelation of what this piece means.

Memorizing these verses has been a lifeline for me. Practice reciting them over yourself every morning and whenever you face trials or temptation.

# 273 | Beware the Loveless Friend

> *I know that my redeemer lives, and that in the end*
> *he will stand on the earth.*
>
> **— JOB 19:25**

The book of Job is an ancient text that offers a master class in how to respond to suffering. Job was a wealthy man with a large family, until his donkeys, oxen, and camels were stolen, his servants were killed, and his son's house was knocked down by a wind, killing all of Job's family. Then he developed sores all over his body! In his agony, three "friends" came and told him everything was his fault and that he must have secret, unconfessed sins. They were wrong. Job maintained his innocence and eventually saw redemption from God.

# 274 | When Love Is Work

> *For we are taking pains to do what is right, not only*
> *in the eyes of the Lord but also in the eyes of man.*
>
> **— 2 CORINTHIANS 8:21**

When we are young and immature, obedience doesn't come naturally to us. Being told what to do (and how) chafes us. It takes time to recognize that we really are a bit inconsistent in our efforts and that God's ways are truly better than ours. During these years, love is work. It requires intentionally dying to ourselves and learning to see the people around us the way God sees them. As our eyes open to the worth of others, loving them becomes natural.

# 275 | When Love Becomes Normal

> *For the entire law is fulfilled in keeping this one command: "Love your neighbor as yourself."*
>
> **— GALATIANS 5:14**

At the heart of the Jesus-centered life are two important truths: (1) We have always been loved by God, and nothing could make him love us more, and (2) our belovedness should affect the way we treat others. You'll know that maturity of faith has come when—without even trying—your daily life is a blessing to everyone around you, and your heart is at peace with God and yourself. This kind of life sums up the entire law. It takes time, but it's possible for love to become normal.

# 276 | God's Covenant with Us

> *"As for me, this is my covenant with them," says the LORD. "My Spirit, who is on you, will not depart from you, and my words that I have put in your mouth will always be on your lips, on the lips of your children and on the lips of their descendants—from this time on and forever," says the LORD.*
>
> **— ISAIAH 59:21**

This passage boggles my mind. Here's my paraphrase: "I, God, make this guarantee to you and all your descendants: My Holy Spirit is in you and will never leave you, which means righteousness and love will flow out of your life every day until the end of time." Isn't that wild?

## 277 | Hearing from God

> *Whether you turn to the right or to the left,*
> *your ears will hear a voice behind*
> *you, saying, "This is the way; walk in it."*
>
> **— ISAIAH 30:21**

When love is work, we need constant guidance from the Spirit to stay in the way that transforms us and others. As love takes deeper root, we find the boundaries moving further and further out. A wise and mature man looks like the picture of freedom yet knows instinctively how fragile the hearts around him are. In your youth, ask God to give you clear guidance. As you mature, don't be surprised when the guidance begins to fade; God trusts you and the choices you'll make.

## 278 | Qualified for Rescue

> *This poor man called, and the LORD heard him;*
> *he saved him out of all his troubles.*
>
> **— PSALM 34:6**

Calling out for help is still difficult for me. When sawing wood, I will build a complicated jig to avoid asking someone to assist me. My issue is not that I think I am unworthy of help but that I don't want to inconvenience anyone. Here's a paradox: The neediness that I worry bothers others (including God) is exactly what brings us together in fellowship and community. The more I need God, the more he comes to my rescue, which he enjoys doing because it means we share time together.

# 279 | The Monkey Trap

> *The Lord is not slow in keeping his promise, as some understand slowness. Instead he is patient with you, not wanting anyone to perish, but everyone to come to repentance.*
>
> **— 2 PETER 3:9**

God longs for every person to turn toward him so that he can heal their brokenness, but we clutch our shame like it's all we have. We're like the proverbial monkey with its fist caught in the jar; the only way to get the thing we want is to let go of it. God waits patiently while our hearts and fingers surrender. I take great hope in the thought that God's patience will outlast even the hardest of hearts.

# 280 | Space and Time

> *"I am the Alpha and the Omega," says the Lord God, "who is, and who was, and who is to come, the Almighty."*
>
> **— REVELATION 1:8**

C. S. Lewis once said that if time is a straight line along which we travel, then God is the paper the line is drawn upon. God gave us the dimensions of space and time, but he is unhindered by them. He can insert himself into our reality whenever and however he pleases, so long as it doesn't violate his nature of love. Although it boggles my mind, I take great comfort in the knowledge that he is before, in, and after all things, holding them all together.

## 281 | The Father of All

> *He tends his flock like a shepherd: He gathers*
> *the lambs in his arms and carries them close to his*
> *heart; he gently leads those that have young.*
>
> **— ISAIAH 40:11**

The ancient Greeks could not conceive that an almighty creator could have anything to do with our daily lives. I admit that I have struggled with this sometimes myself. The truth is that God Almighty not only knows my name, but he is also intimately involved in my life and the life of everything else he created. He cares for me and my children, and he cares for the sheep, birds, plants, and everything else, too. He really is the Father of all.

## 282 | When Others Pick Fights

> *Then Asa called to the LORD his God and said,*
> *"LORD, there is no one like you to help the powerless*
> *against the mighty. Help us, LORD our God,*
> *for we rely on you, and in your name we have come*
> *against this vast army. LORD, you are our*
> *God; do not let mere mortals prevail against you."*
>
> **— 2 CHRONICLES 14:11**

Asa was king of Judah (the southern part of Israel) around 900 BCE. His reign was peaceful for decades until a vast army attacked them. If you've tried to be a man of peace and righteousness but others keep trying to pick fights, Asa understands. He called on God to defend them, and you and I can, too.

# 283 | Either Follow Jesus or Please Others

*Am I now trying to win the approval of human beings, or of God? Or am I trying to please people? If I were still trying to please people, I would not be a servant of Christ.*

**— GALATIANS 1:10**

I've wasted years of my life seeking the approval of others. The apostle Paul offers a word of caution: You cannot follow Jesus and try to please other people at the same time. It just doesn't work. If you, too, struggle with people-pleasing, consider what this says about your unmet needs, your conflict style, your sense of safety, and your trust in God. Jesus can free you of this bondage.

# 284 | Bit by Bit

*This is what the LORD says—your Redeemer, the Holy One of Israel: "I am the LORD your God, who teaches you what is best for you, who directs you in the way you should go."*

**— ISAIAH 48:17**

Consider how your knowledge, wisdom, and skill stack up against the one who exists outside the bonds of space and time, who created life itself, from whom nothing is hidden. Do we really think following our own plans will work out better than trusting his guidance? It's kind of crazy how stubborn we are. I often wish God would reveal everything to me upfront, but I guess I wouldn't have to trust him if he did.

# 285 | An Honest History

> *By the rivers of Babylon we sat and wept*
> *when we remembered Zion.*
>
> **— PSALM 137:1**

They say history is written by the victors. Since most people tend to embellish their own stories, we must take the details they left us with a grain of salt. Consequently, if you find a story that doesn't shine well on the victors, it's much more likely to be true. That's one of the things I love about the Hebrew scriptures: They are brutally honest about their own mistakes and the failures of their heroes. It's often wiser to sit by the river and weep than to worship a temporary hero.

# 286 | Who Is the Evil One?

> *But the Lord is faithful, and he will strengthen you*
> *and protect you from the evil one.*
>
> **— 2 THESSALONIANS 3:3**

I spent many of my early Christian years terrified of the devil. The guy with the pitchfork haunted my dreams, and I blamed him for most of my mistakes. Reading a passage like this, I would thank God for protecting me from the Prince of Darkness. An examination of the language behind "evil one," however, reveals that Paul is talking about anyone who does wicked things, not some devil. God promises to establish us, make us firm, and guard us against evildoers. That's a good word.

# 287 | Becoming a Martyr

> *Therefore we do not lose heart. Though outwardly we are wasting away, yet inwardly we are being renewed day by day.*
>
> **— 2 CORINTHIANS 4:16**

Following Jesus always results in death. For some, it's a figurative ego death, while for others, it's their actual physical death. Paul, who wrote this verse, had Christians imprisoned and killed before meeting Jesus. By the end of the fourth century, countless believers faced torture, brutality, and death alongside Rome's criminals. Most of us today will not face the martyrdom of our bodies, but we must all take up our crosses and die to ourselves, trusting in God.

# 288 | Persecution Brings Beauty

> *For our light and momentary troubles are achieving for us an eternal glory that far outweighs them all. So we fix our eyes not on what is seen, but on what is unseen, since what is seen is temporary, but what is unseen is eternal.*
>
> **— 2 CORINTHIANS 4:17–18**

The apostles were being murdered for proclaiming Jesus, and Paul called it "light and momentary troubles." Today, many so-called Christians claim religious persecution whenever a difference in worldviews stops them from doing all they want to do. Power and privilege have dulled us, but persecution will bring forth glory, the beautiful truth of who we are in Christ.

# 289 | Resisting Entitlement

> *In your relationships with one another, have the same mindset as Christ Jesus: Who, being in very nature God, did not consider equality with God something to be used to his own advantage; rather, he made himself nothing by taking the very nature of a servant, being made in human likeness.*
>
> **— PHILIPPIANS 2:5-7**

Whenever someone treats me poorly, I try to bring myself back to this: Jesus was God-made-flesh and did not use the power or the privilege of it for his own gain. He refused any sense of entitlement. Just writing that sickens me—I feel entitled so much of the time. We must resist this temptation and serve others humbly, just like Jesus.

# 290 | The Path of Exaltation

> *Therefore God exalted him to the highest place and gave him the name that is above every name, that at the name of Jesus every knee should bow, in heaven and on earth and under the earth, and every tongue acknowledge that Jesus Christ is Lord, to the glory of God the Father.*
>
> **— PHILIPPIANS 2:9-11**

In response to Jesus's humility, the Father honored him above all others, promising that everyone will eventually bow their knee to him. Do you want to be exalted and praised before others? If so, do what Jesus did: Take up your cross and die horrifically to rescue and redeem the people killing you. That's the path to exaltation. Oorah.

# 291 | What Else Matters?

> *What, then, shall we say in response to these things?*
> *If God is for us, who can be against us?*
>
> **— ROMANS 8:31**

This passage has been rattling around in my head since I was ten years old. I used to think of it in terms of bullies and bad guys; if God was with me, those guys couldn't beat me up. As I sit with it today, I'm thinking bigger. If God—who is all powerful and knows all of us inside and out, including our fantasies, fixations, and failures—is with us and for us, then what else matters? Let's just go and explore life and love on this beautiful planet.

# 292 | A Rhythm of Reset

> *There remains, then, a Sabbath-rest for the people*
> *of God; for anyone who enters God's rest also*
> *rests from their works, just as God did from his.*
>
> **— HEBREWS 4:9–10**

Sabbath is an overlooked spiritual rhythm in most of North America. We like to work hard and party hard, trusting ourselves and no one else. Sabbath provokes our fears and frustrations. It requires us to stop working, stop checking our phones, stop making money, stop entertaining ourselves, stop preparing for the unexpected, stop filling every moment with something, and just be. Just trust that for these moments, God and us are enough. Whether you enjoy a Sabbath weekly or sporadically, it's an important rhythm of reset.

# 293 | A Parent Who Heals

*See what great love the Father has lavished
on us, that we should be called children of God!
And that is what we are!*

**— 1 JOHN 3:1A**

I once met an author I appreciate, and I even had dinner with him, his wife, and his children. I noticed how confident and at peace their children were. It seemed no great surprise to them that an adult they had never met would be interested in their artwork, their games, their stories, and their perspectives on life. Healthy kids anticipate positive engagement and dignity. No wonder God longs to father and mother us as his own precious children.

# 294 | All Means All

*The LORD Almighty will prepare a feast of rich food
for all peoples.... On this mountain he will destroy the
shroud that enfolds all peoples, the sheet that covers
all nations; he will swallow up death forever.*

**— ISAIAH 25:6–8A**

I grew up believing that only a few would make it into heaven, the rest being tortured in hell forever. The longer I spend with God and scripture, the harder it gets to believe this story. I don't know if you can reject love forever, and if you can, I don't know what happens to you, but I'm convinced God wants to rescue and redeem everyone and everything he made.

# 295 | Justice Is Good News

> *Yet the LORD longs to be gracious to you; therefore he will rise up to show you compassion. For the LORD is a God of justice. Blessed are all who wait for him!*
>
> **— ISAIAH 30:18**

I grew up feeling evil and dirty. I feared that the more God got to know me, the more likely he would discover how gross I was, and the hammer would finally fall. When I started to learn that I was more broken than bad, my fear of justice dissolved. Justice is only bad news for the oppressor. It's the best news for everyone else! If you've been waiting on God for deliverance, know that he is coming.

# 296 | How to Get Yourself Killed

> *But Stephen, full of the Holy Spirit, looked up to heaven and saw the glory of God, and Jesus standing at the right hand of God. "Look," he said, "I see heaven open and the Son of Man standing at the right hand of God."*
>
> **— ACTS 7:55–56**

Stephen was the first person martyred for proclaiming the good news of Jesus. He stood up in front of the religious Jewish elite, the very men entrusted with caring for God's chosen people, and gave an honest assessment of the condition of their hearts. Rather than accept this rebuke, they lashed out in rage and stoned him to death. Following Jesus usually offends the religious establishment.

# 297 | Rethinking the Fear of God

> *But the eyes of the LORD are on those who fear him,*
> *on those whose hope is in his unfailing love.*
>
> **— PSALM 33:18**

Fear of God is like shorthand for "awareness of the consequences of our selfishness with adoring thankfulness for God's gracious healing of our brokenness." The more time you spend with Jesus, the more this "fear of God" develops in you. It is very little like the bodily emotion of fear, which brings adrenaline and cortisol. Fear of God brings freedom, holiness, joy, and life. Place your hope in the unfailing love of God. It's worth it.

# 298 | Joy Factory

> *Nehemiah said, "Go and enjoy choice food and sweet*
> *drinks, and send some to those who have nothing*
> *prepared. This day is holy to our Lord. Do not grieve,*
> *for the joy of the LORD is your strength."*
>
> **— NEHEMIAH 8:10**

Some of the exiled Israelites had returned from Babylon and began restoring their practices of worship. Ezra, the priest, read aloud the law of Moses, which caused the people to weep because they hadn't been able to follow it for seventy years. But Ezra and Nehemiah explained that this was a time to celebrate. As the people shared food with one another, it says, "They now understood" (verse 12). The righteousness of God is always meant to produce joy.

# 299 | Cultivating the Spirit

> *And in him you too are being built together to become a dwelling in which God lives by his Spirit.*
>
> **— EPHESIANS 2:22**

One of the things about the Christian message that is rather unique is that God makes his dwelling place among us. He's not far off in heaven; he's right here. But his indwelling is communal and procedural. Following Jesus is not a one-man show; we need genuine community, which takes time to develop. Like a seed that must be planted and watered, God's presence is given to us for free, but to experience the fullness of God, we must cultivate it and nurture it among us. The Spirit transforms us as we cultivate room for him.

# 300 | Even in Death . . .

> *Where can I go from your Spirit? Where can I flee from your presence? If I go up to the heavens, you are there; if I make my bed in the depths, you are there.*
>
> **— PSALM 139:7–8**

Psalm 139 is my favorite psalm, and this verse always boggles my mind. It's not that strange of a concept that we would find God in the heavens . . . but the depths? The Hebrew word is *Sheol*, the place of the dead. The Greeks called it Hades. And the psalmist says God is found there, too. I guess all the cosmos, in every dimension and frame of reality, really does radiate the presence of God.

# 301 | The Fire That Purifies

*If your enemy is hungry, give him food to eat; if he is thirsty, give him water to drink. In doing this, you will heap burning coals on his head, and the LORD will reward you.*

**— PROVERBS 25:21-22**

The image of fire or burning coals comes up fairly often in scripture. It can reflect different things, but it most typically represents a process of purification. If God touches you with fire, it is not to hurt you but to cleanse you of anything that is not of love. By loving our enemies, we partner with God, enabling his burning coals of purifying redemption to be poured out upon them.

# 302 | The Fate of the Wicked

*Meanwhile, Saul was still breathing out murderous threats against the Lord's disciples.... As he neared Damascus on his journey, suddenly a light from heaven flashed around him. He fell to the ground and heard a voice say to him, "Saul, Saul, why do you persecute me?"*

**— ACTS 9:1A, 3-4**

Loving our enemies is what brings true justice into the world. Burning coals are poured out, and evildoers are confronted with the reality of what they have done and the forgiveness and grace that God offers. Their burden is to carry that knowledge in humility. The fate of the wicked is to be redeemed and to know it. This is true justice.

# 303 | The Pit Isn't Always Our Fault

> *I waited patiently for the LORD; he turned to me and heard my cry. He lifted me out of the slimy pit, out of the mud and mire; he set my feet on a rock and gave me a firm place to stand.*
>
> **— PSALM 40:1–2**

During the COVID-19 pandemic, I began to drink more. Life was unpleasant and unpredictable, and the stimulating and depressive effects of coffee and alcohol gave me an agreeable measure of control over my life. They also made me jittery and emotionally unstable, and I gained weight. I had dug a pit for myself when all I was trying to do was survive. Thankfully, there was grace for that, too.

# 304 | No More Begging

> *For we do not have a high priest who is unable to empathize with our weaknesses, but we have one who has been tempted in every way, just as we are—yet he did not sin. Let us then approach God's throne of grace with confidence, so that we may receive mercy and find grace to help us in our time of need.*
>
> **— HEBREWS 4:15–16**

We are invited to approach God boldly and confidently, like an expectant child going to their generous parents. The calculus on this is that Jesus was tempted in all the same ways we are, so God understands what it's like being human. Thanks to Jesus, we don't ever have to go to the Father cap in hand.

> *Now to each one the manifestation of the Spirit is given for the common good. To one there is given through the Spirit a message of wisdom, to another a message of knowledge by means of the same Spirit, to another faith by the same Spirit, to another gifts of healing by that one Spirit, to another miraculous powers, to another prophecy, to another distinguishing between spirits, to another speaking in different kinds of tongues, and to still another the interpretation of tongues. All these are the work of one and the same Spirit, and he distributes them to each one, just as he determines.*
>
> **— 1 CORINTHIANS 12:7-11**

The Holy Spirit is given to everyone, and it manifests goodness in our lives. As we cultivate more room for the Spirit to work in us, we experience a more divine life. All these gifts—prophecy, healing, radical faith, speaking other languages—are given for the sake of those around us. They're presents that demonstrate the heart of God to the world and are meant to be regifted.

## Live Out the Word

Does your tradition encourage and release the gifts of the Holy Spirit, or are you wary of that? Why might this be?

Have you observed one of these gifts in operation before, whether in your life or someone else's? Does one of them resonate more with you than the others?

Ask the Holy Spirit to fill you anew and give you something to regift to those around you.

# 306 | The Hope of Suffering

> *We also glory in our sufferings, because we know*
> *that suffering produces perseverance;*
> *perseverance, character; and character, hope.*
>
> **— ROMANS 5:3–4**

As we've discussed, glory is the true nature of something. Paul explains to the Jesus followers in Rome that they can expect suffering to help reveal their true character and nature. Going through hard things helps us learn patience and perseverance; it increases our tolerance and helps us handle more without losing our cool. That process buffs out the flaws in our character, making us people of peace with a greater capacity for love. Discovering that love flows out of us in hard times is a great source of hope.

# 307 | The Lessons of Trust

> *The LORD is good, a refuge in times of trouble.*
> *He cares for those who trust in him.*
>
> **— NAHUM 1:7**

A few years ago, I quit my salaried job to become a full-time writer. We didn't have any funds in reserve, so it was a big leap of faith. It took over three years for my writing income to start paying the bills, and God miraculously paid our mortgage and other expenses every month. We never knew where it would come from; it usually arrived at the last moment with a few dollars to spare. But God did that for three years, and it changed our understanding of trust.

# 308 | Living Hope

*Praise be to the God and Father of our Lord Jesus Christ! In his great mercy he has given us new birth into a living hope through the resurrection of Jesus Christ from the dead.*

**— 1 PETER 1:3**

Jesus didn't come to launch the Christian religion. What he was doing was so much bigger than religion, tribalism, or nationalism. Jesus was revealing God, restoring the world, and establishing a new kind of life on this planet. As Jesus followers, we're not called to be good Christians who change the world; we're called to be the world already changed by Jesus. Of course, that kind of life will be infectious.

# 309 | Cultivating Inner Rest

*Truly my soul finds rest in God; my salvation comes from him.*

**— PSALM 62:1**

A few years ago, I went on my first silent retreat. My friend and I drove to an abbey in upstate New York and spent two days walking, sitting, eating, and praying in total silence. We broke silence only to chant the Psalms with the monks four times a day. The setting was tranquil and peaceful, and by dedicating this time to silent pursuit of God, I inadvertently accessed a space of inner rest inside myself. I can turn there now most anytime and find peace in the midst of my busy day.

# 310 | A Glorious Inheritance

*I pray that the eyes of your heart may be
enlightened in order that you may know the hope
to which he has called you, the riches
of his glorious inheritance in his holy people.*

**— EPHESIANS 1:18**

My credit card comes with a range of benefits, including my favorite: access to airport lounges. I didn't know I had this until just before the pandemic, so I haven't used it much. Similarly, it is possible to follow Jesus and not realize all the benefits available to us. These are not benefits of power or prestige but of confidence, grace, and hope. May our eyes be opened to this glorious inheritance.

# 311 | Older than Steel

*Before the mountains were born or you
brought forth the whole world, from everlasting
to everlasting you are God.*

**— PSALM 90:2**

I enjoy getting out into nature to meditate on God. Go find an old tree and put your hand on it. Think back 150 years and consider that this tree drank sunlight during two world wars, and it didn't need anything from you to do so. Find a slab of rock somewhere and put your hand on that. Consider that it's been a part of this world for longer than steel has been. Before all of that even, God was here, and God was looking forward to getting to know you.

# 312 | Bittersweet Respect

> *But we have this treasure in jars of clay to show that this all-surpassing power is from God and not from us.*
>
> **— 2 CORINTHIANS 4:7**

I have observed a few wise and caring old men be pricked in their hearts with grief over their sins in their later years. Many of their regrets seemed minor trifles to me, things I wouldn't even notice given the clamor of my big, glaring failures. This is the paradox of moving toward God: The more we mature in love, the more aware we become of our failure to love. There is still no shame, only a bittersweet respect for all of God's gifts and the fragility of these clay jars.

# 313 | So Many Reasons to Be Afraid

> *I sought the LORD, and he answered me; he delivered me from all my fears.*
>
> **— PSALM 34:4**

I was not an overly fearful child, but I couldn't wait to become an adult because I thought grown-ups were never afraid of anything. Now that I'm here myself, it seems I only have more things to be afraid of. I would rather not admit to any of this, but once again the honesty of the psalmist uncovers me. I've heard that scripture includes some form of the phrase "do not be afraid" over 350 times. Clearly, God understands how much our lives can be driven by fear without him.

## 314 | Let's Go

> *Praise be to the God and Father of our Lord Jesus Christ, who has blessed us in the heavenly realms with every spiritual blessing in Christ.*
>
> **— EPHESIANS 1:3**

There are some Christian traditions that outlaw drinking, playing cards, dancing, speaking in tongues, making love for pleasure, going to the movies, getting tattoos, smoking cigars, and much more. I respect the personal piety of anyone who makes such a choice for God, but I don't see much of that asceticism in the life of Jesus. He has given us all the blessings, natural and spiritual, and invited us to model what freedom and joy look like. I say, let's go.

## 315 | One Love, One People

> *For we were all baptized by one Spirit so as to form one body—whether Jews or Gentiles, slave or free—and we were all given the one Spirit to drink.*
>
> **— 1 CORINTHIANS 12:13**

One of the massive ramifications of God's outpouring of the Spirit onto all peoples, inviting all humanity to partner with him in spreading love to the world, is that it overcomes any kind of racial or tribal boundary. Followers of Jesus should expect and rejoice to see brothers and sisters of all skin colors and identities at their side. If you find yourself surrounded mostly by one skin color, ask God to broaden the palette in your life.

# 316 | A Much Better Government

> *For to us a child is born, to us a son is given,*
> *and the government will be on his shoulders. And*
> *he will be called Wonderful Counselor,*
> *Mighty God, Everlasting Father, Prince of Peace.*
>
> **— ISAIAH 9:6**

This passage is one of my favorites. It calls to my mind the poverty of Jesus's birth, the scourging of his shoulders, his crucifixion, and his gift of peace to us. But Isaiah goes further, linking this promised savior to the Holy Spirit (Wonderful Counselor) and the Father Almighty (Mighty God, Everlasting Father). Isaiah was prophesying the Trinity before Jesus had even come. This is a very good government.

# 317 | Doing the Work

> *Therefore, my dear brothers and sisters, stand firm.*
> *Let nothing move you. Always give yourselves*
> *fully to the work of the Lord, because you know that*
> *your labor in the Lord is not in vain.*
>
> **— 1 CORINTHIANS 15:58**

I've been a pastor for some time, and I can tell you it's often hard work. I feel like quitting a lot. I know I'm free to quit without shame or condemnation, but then I wouldn't have the satisfaction of having stood firm and watched the Spirit work around me. The freedom that we have in God does not conflict with the call to do the work. It enables and motivates the work.

# 318 | Sometimes We Slip

> *When I said, "My foot is slipping," your unfailing love,*
> *Lord, supported me.*
>
> **— PSALM 94:18**

When I talk about the hardships of life, I am not speaking in the abstract. Between being a dad and a foster parent, pastoring in a local church, writing books about the inner life, and trying to love my wife well—while managing my sometimes fragile mental and emotional health—I know what hopelessness and despair feel like. I imagine you do, too. Sometimes my feet slip, and I turn to false comforts. Thankfully, God saves me as much fom my circumstances as from how I attempt to deal with them.

# 319 | Mystical Perfection

> *For we are God's handiwork, created in*
> *Christ Jesus to do good works,*
> *which God prepared in advance for us to do.*
>
> **— EPHESIANS 2:10**

This new kind of human that we are is God's masterpiece, God's crowning achievement. The dirt and dust of our creation now reside inside Jesus himself. We are free to do good for the world, and our good works flow out of the divine spark that lives in us. The spark in us seeks the spark in all created things, triggering a beautiful dance. If this sounds rather mystical, that's because it is! God created life that was just like him: beautiful, powerful, and freely in love with creation.

# 320 | The Inward Journey

*The human spirit is the lamp of the LORD that
shed light on one's inmost being.*

**— PROVERBS 20:27**

The burning core of your emotions, the mansion of your
memories, the offices of rational thought, and your raw
survival instincts all try to take the wheel in your life. Only
your true spirit, the undiminished self made in the image of
God, can bring calm, clear alignment to your inmost being.
This is the part of you that knows Jesus is always here and
always bringing light. Learning to identify and listen to your
inner parts requires time and compassionate attention. It's a
path of meditation that God will lead you down if you want.

# 321 | We Create the Idols

*I will sprinkle clean water on you, and you
will be clean; I will cleanse you from
all your impurities and from all your idols.*

**— EZEKIEL 36:25**

It seems we often chase things that we are tricked into
believing will soothe our pain and bring us joy–that career,
that relationship, that recognition, that trophy. None
of these things is worthy of the devotion of a made-in-
God's-image human being. Chasing them hurts us because
it denies the godly sufficiency we have right here in ourselves. Obsessions are a form of idolatry. It is good and
right to repent of all our idolatries and let Jesus make us
new once again.

# 322 | Creation Yearns for Love

> *For the creation waits in eager expectation for the children of God to be revealed.*
>
> **— ROMANS 8:19**

If we could understand the language of trees, rocks, and rivers, I think we would hear their longing for the time when humans loved and cared for them and when God walked among them each day. I really do believe that every human—and all creation itself—yearns for love-made-real to walk and talk with them. Of course, they may not all know it. To the extent that we take up our crosses and walk in loving solidarity with the hurting world around us, we are revealed as the children of God.

# 323 | The Hope of Glory

> *To them God has chosen to make known among the Gentiles the glorious riches of this mystery, which is Christ in you, the hope of glory.*
>
> **— COLOSSIANS 1:27**

The Hebrew scriptures weave a long story of God's promise of redemption for all humanity. This is good and true. But the means and outcome of that deliverance no one could conceive of until it was revealed. Not only would God save us all, but God would also live inside us, forever sustaining, informing, and transforming us and everyone around us. Our deepest truth is Jesus in us, a profound mystery that not even the prophets who predicted it could have really understood.

# 324 | Hope in His Coming

> *Therefore, with minds that are alert and fully*
> *sober, set your hope on the grace to be brought to you*
> *when Jesus Christ is revealed at his coming.*
>
> **— 1 PETER 1:13**

One of the core hopes of those who follow Jesus is that he will come again and be revealed to all creation. It is possible to fixate on the return of Jesus in an unhealthy way, and I think that's why writers such as Peter and Paul used the language of hope. Hope is nebulous and hard to pin down. It floats away, then it taps you on the shoulder. Hope isn't a concrete timeline, but hope is real, and hope is good.

# 325 | Hope Won't Fail

> *And hope does not put us to shame, because*
> *God's love has been poured out into our hearts through*
> *the Holy Spirit, who has been given to us.*
>
> **— ROMANS 5:5**

Phew. That's good news. The deposit, or down payment, that God has given us, the security, the bond, is his Holy Spirit. Jesus isn't going to run off into other dimensions, leaving us here on this broken earth. He has left his Spirit with us, and you can be sure Jesus will come back for it. And the truth is even better than my wordplay. God's love is here in us, and our hope in his presence and his return will not be disappointed. Thank God for that.

# 326 | Set You Free

> *To the Jews who had believed him, Jesus said, "If you hold to my teaching, you are really my disciples. Then you will know the truth, and the truth will set you free."*
>
> **— JOHN 8:31–32**

Here's a strange and concerning thing. According to John, being a devout Jew and even believing in Jesus does not guarantee that you know truth or have freedom. The phrase that is translated "hold to my teaching" comes from the Greek *meinēte en tō logō*. Abide in the Word-made-flesh. Remain in Jesus, the embodied expression of all that God wants and is, and then you will know truth, and it will set you free.

# 327 | Justice Is Light

> *And if you spend yourselves in behalf of the hungry and satisfy the needs of the oppressed, then your light will rise in the darkness, and your night will become like the noonday.*
>
> **— ISAIAH 58:10**

This passage reads like a social justice spoken word mash-up of James 1:27 and John 1:5. Light versus darkness and blackest night versus noonday are powerful poetic pictures of reversal. When the children of God pour out the divine love within them on behalf of the broken and needy, there is a grand reversal where justice triumphs over oppression. Not bad for something written 2,750 years ago.

> *In him we have redemption through his blood, the forgiveness of sins, in accordance with the riches of God's grace that he lavished on us. With all wisdom and understanding, he made known to us the mystery of his will according to his good pleasure, which he purposed in Christ, to be put into effect when the times reach their fulfillment—to bring unity to all things in heaven and on earth under Christ.*
>
> **— EPHESIANS 1:7–10**

When God made the universe, where do you think he put it? If God was all there was and our dimensions of time and space didn't exist yet, what do you think he wove it all from, and where did he hang it? Paul returns to this point over and over again: All things are summed up in Jesus. It seems to me that God made the cosmos right there inside of himself and Jesus is the proof. The forgiveness, redemption, and cleansing he accomplished were absolutely necessary but aren't the point. The point is rediscovering what Jesus knew: the truth of our location and our identity.

## Live Out the Word

If you knew that you were inside of God at all times, how would that change your life?

What do you think "bring unity to all things" means? Do you interpret this the same way I do? (You don't have to, by the way.)

Ask the Holy Spirit to give you a glimpse of the metaphysical nature of reality itself in all its dimensions.

# 329 | Imprinted on Our Hearts

> *I will put my law in their minds and write it on their hearts. I will be their God, and they will be my people.... For I will forgive their wickedness and will remember their sins no more.*
>
> **— JEREMIAH 31:33B, 34B**

The prophet Jeremiah spoke what was to become our reality. Thanks to the Holy Spirit dwelling within us, we have the law of love imprinted on our hearts and minds. The same Holy Spirit reminds us of our forgiven-ness and how welcome we are with the Father. What was only a shadow of a dream for the people of Israel is now our reality. You can lean into that good news.

# 330 | Painful Hope

> *Hope deferred makes the heart sick, but a longing fulfilled is a tree of life.*
>
> **— PROVERBS 13:12**

One of the things I love about scripture is its power to reach beyond time and culture and hit me square in the chest, like this verse, my favorite from the book of Proverbs. Hope deferred makes the heart sick. Yeah, it does. Whether your dream is of a spouse, a house, kids, better health, a promotion, or anything else, having your hopes delayed repeatedly is costly. It impacts the wiring of your brain and changes the way you think. It's okay to be real with God about that as you wait in painful hope.

# 331 | Life in the Middle

> *We are hard pressed on every side, but not crushed; perplexed, but not in despair; persecuted, but not abandoned; struck down, but not destroyed.*
>
> **— 2 CORINTHIANS 4:8-9**

In the early years of my faith, when following Jesus meant prosperity and victory, I couldn't readily identify with this passage. A few more years has taught me otherwise, and today I find great solidarity in these words. A long obedience to the way of love will indeed press you, though not destroy you. Living in this state of tension, caring for the world God loves, aching for the dawn of a new reality isn't easy, but there is goodness here, too.

# 332 | Scandalous Expression

> *The LORD your God is with you, the Mighty Warrior who saves. He will take great delight in you; in his love he will no longer rebuke you, but will rejoice over you with singing.*
>
> **— ZEPHANIAH 3:17**

Scripture is full of the wildest, most scandalous descriptions of God's passionate love for us and of our worship for him. King David, the mighty warrior, was also a poet and musician, and he once danced naked in the streets of Jerusalem. This passage portrays God in the same kind of light. I don't know how we ended up with so many Christian men who are dour and unemotional, but I say we ditch that nonsense.

# 333 | It's All a Gift

> *But because of his great love for us, God, who is*
> *rich in mercy, made us alive with Christ*
> *even when we were dead in transgressions—it is*
> *by grace you have been saved.*
>
> **— EPHESIANS 2:4–5**

If you asked anyone about their salvation two thousand years ago, they would tell you it was based on their genealogy, their ethnic group, or their sacrifices. If you ask someone today, they'll typically tell you it's based on their good works or their faith in God, if they even understand the question. These answers fall short of the simple truth: We have salvation because God gave it to us when we couldn't even ask for it.

# 334 | Until You Croak

> *My flesh and my heart may fail, but God is the strength*
> *of my heart and my portion forever.*
>
> **— PSALM 73:26**

This body of yours is going to waste away and die one day. If you've gone around the sun twenty-five times, the decay has already begun. Every day you are getting older and more wrinkly, and eventually your heart will stop, and your atoms will be returned to the earth God made. And then you will nourish the trees and grass, maybe even providing shade for a new generation, while you await the return of Jesus and the transformation of the cosmos. Until then, God will remain your strength and your reward.

# 335 | The Jesus Manifesto

> *He has shown you, O mortal, what is good. And what does the LORD require of you? To act justly and to love mercy and to walk humbly with your God.*
>
> **— MICAH 6:8**

To act justly is, at the very least, to refuse to oppress, exploit, or manipulate other people or the earth. To love mercy is, at the very least, to appreciate the power of compassion, kindness, and grace. To live humbly with God is, at the very least, to not obsess over wealth, nice things, being the best at everything, or becoming famous and to not think any more—or less—of yourself than God does. That's the Jesus manifesto: justice, mercy, humility.

# 336 | What Happens to One . . .

> *There is neither Jew nor Gentile, neither slave nor free, nor is there male and female, for you are all one in Christ Jesus.*
>
> **— GALATIANS 3:28**

In contrast to the way of Jesus, people have often weaponized the Bible. The one who says "Love your enemies" stands in opposition to those who would use scripture to justify enslavement, to condemn mixed-race marriage, to oppress immigrants, or to treat people differently because of their sexuality. In Jesus, all ethnic, racial, and gender barriers are dissolved even while distinctiveness is celebrated. We are all one, and what happens to anyone affects everyone.

## 337 | The Ways of the Spirit

> So he said to me, "This is the word of the LORD
> to Zerubbabel: 'Not by might nor by power, but by
> my Spirit,' says the LORD Almighty."
>
> **— ZECHARIAH 4:6**

As we near the end of our year together, this passage is a good reminder that the way of love isn't followed by sheer determination. We can't live the others-centered life that Jesus showed us in our own might. We do it by surrendering to his Spirit within us and letting him animate our actions, guide our steps, and move our hearts. It's as counter-cultural today as it has ever been. Such are the ways of the Spirit.

## 338 | Be a Man

> Be on your guard; stand firm in the faith;
> be courageous; be strong.
>
> **— 1 CORINTHIANS 16:13**

On the playgrounds of my childhood, being told to be a man implied that you were weak, childish, and feminine, all things most young boys didn't want said of them. Men were brave, strong, even dominating. Care to guess what Paul literally wrote here, which we translate "be courageous"? He used the Greek word for males and turned it into a verb. "Be manly," he said, in regard to your faith. Although much of masculinity has acquired toxic baggage, being a man and following Jesus are not incompatible. May we all explore that more.

# 339 | Veiled Hearts

> *To this day the same veil remains when the old covenant is read. It has not been removed, because only in Christ is it taken away. Even to this day when Moses is read, a veil covers their hearts. But whenever anyone turns to the Lord, the veil is taken away.*
>
> **— 2 CORINTHIANS 3:14B–16**

When we read the Bible without the Holy Spirit's guidance, our hearts and minds are veiled, and we can't see God for who he is. What that usually results in is religious legalism driven by fear of punishment from a violent, retributive God. When we see Jesus, however, we see God clearly, and the whole story changes.

# 340 | His Wrath

> *Lᴏʀᴅ, I have heard of your fame; I stand in awe of your deeds, Lᴏʀᴅ. Repeat them in our day, in our time make them known; in wrath remember mercy.*
>
> **— HABAKKUK 3:2**

Recall that anger is the emotional response to being violated or blocked (including when that happens to someone we care about). If God gets angry, it is because his beloved children have been violated and the way of love he intended for everyone has been blocked. His wrath is nothing like that of a human blinded by rage; it is pure, high-intensity advocacy. It defeats darkness, sets captives free, and brings oppressors to their knees in devastating humility.

# 341 | Transformational Truth

> *Grace, mercy and peace from God the Father and from Jesus Christ, the Father's Son, will be with us in truth and love.*
>
> **— 2 JOHN 1:3**

I used to fear God's truth because I thought the truth about myself was all bad and God would be disgusted. But God is love and his Spirit is truth, and what the truth does is set us free. But as Dr. Fieldstone explains in *Ted Lasso*, it might piss us off first. Truth invites us to humility and adoration of the God who knows everything about us and yet loves us. Grace, mercy, and peace for all are made possible only as we are transformed.

# 342 | Boast in the Lord

> *"But let the one who boasts boast about this: that they have the understanding to know me, that I am the LORD, who exercises kindness, justice and righteousness on earth, for in these I delight," declares the LORD.*
>
> **— JEREMIAH 9:24**

Research suggests that angry conflicts between men turn violent more frequently when there's an audience. I think this relates to our temptation to be proud and boastful. So many of us were conditioned to talk a big game and avoid showing weakness. God invites us to boast in something completely different: that we have enough understanding to know God. I think it's a trap, really.

# 343 | God's Citizenship

> *Consequently, you are no longer foreigners
> and strangers, but fellow citizens with
> God's people and also members of his household.*
>
> **— EPHESIANS 2:19**

I have lived in five different countries, so I know what it feels like to be a stranger. If you've never felt this, try watching a foreign-language film without subtitles. It's not just the meaning of the words that you fail to catch; it's the subtle clues, the glances, the unique things that are simply understood by a given cultural group. Being an outsider is a painfully heavy burden. Not so with God. He calls you a citizen and a member of his own family. You understand his inside jokes.

# 344 | Healing and Strength

> *And the God of all grace, who called you to his
> eternal glory in Christ, after you have
> suffered a little while, will himself restore you
> and make you strong, firm and steadfast.*
>
> **— 1 PETER 5:10**

I hope these reflections on suffering don't scare you. I used to gloss over these passages, until I experienced real hardship and they became rather comforting. Loving and serving others and refusing to live an egocentric life is painful and transformational, and it will provoke other people. They will judge you and attack you, all because your way of love and freedom exposes their lack of it. Trust in God. He will restore you.

# 345 | The Promise of Strength

> *The LORD is the everlasting God, the Creator of the ends of the earth. He will not grow tired or weary, and his understanding no one can fathom. He gives strength to the weary and increases the power of the weak.*
>
> **— ISAIAH 40:28B-29**

A popular trope in science fiction is the extinct alien race who created massive structures in space before dying out. Something about these everlasting artifacts constructed of imperishable metals has always fascinated me. I think it's because God is everlasting, and my mind just can't comprehend it. He doesn't wear out, he doesn't give up, and he never stops pursuing us. His promise of strength is something I really need.

# 346 | Worthy of Our Devotion

> *You are worthy, our Lord and God, to receive glory and honor and power, for you created all things, and by your will they were created and have their being.*
>
> **— REVELATION 4:11**

I can get that God created all things, but the part about having their being in God intrigues me. One philosopher stated that God is less a being among other beings than he is the ground of being itself. Without God, we would all lapse into nonbeing, which is something my mind simply balks at. The first followers of Jesus took a really broad view: God is all in all, personally knowable and worthy of our devotion.

## 347 | Sharing the Vision

> *For prophecy never had its origin in the human will,*
> *but prophets, though human, spoke from*
> *God as they were carried along by the Holy Spirit.*

**— 2 PETER 1:21**

Growing up in the charismatic movement, I saw so many abuses of prophecy that I often wanted nothing to do with it. As I have journeyed with God, however, I've come to recognize the importance of this gift, of how capturing a vision of God's heart of love can give us hope to continue onward. We need prophets to help encourage us, to correct our path at times, and to communicate the love and presence of God when we can't sense it ourselves.

## 348 | Manifest the Work

> *A father to the fatherless, a defender of widows,*
> *is God in his holy dwelling.*

**— PSALM 68:5**

Throughout scripture, God shows a special care for orphans, widows, and foreigners. Mary, Joseph, and Jesus became foreigners in Egypt to avoid being slaughtered by Herod. Later, Mary most likely became a widow herself. As men, traditionally blessed with an extra measure of strength and cultural privilege, we have a duty to care for orphans and defend widows. When we do this in the power of the Holy Spirit and the humility of Jesus, we manifest and exhibit the work that God has always been doing. Now, that is a privilege.

# 349 | Living Free

> *Don't you know that when you offer yourselves to someone as obedient slaves, you are slaves of the one you obey—whether you are slaves to sin, which leads to death, or to obedience, which leads to righteousness?*
>
> **— ROMANS 6:16**

For some, human enslavement might seem like a distant concept, but there are still people alive today whose grandparents were enslaved. When you include forced labor, sexual exploitation, and child marriages, there are more people enslaved today than ever before. As you thank Jesus for setting you free from sin, pray for those still trapped in human exploitation.

# 350 | Light and Life

> *For I take no pleasure in the death of anyone, declares the Sovereign LORD. Repent and live!*
>
> **— EZEKIEL 18:32**

Darkness and death have nothing to do with God. When we turn away from light and life, we find ourselves tormented by death and darkness. This is not a punishment from God; it's simply the outcome of the path we chose, whether we did so intentionally in rebellion or because we were deceived. The Hebrew word that is translated as *repent* means "to turn back" or "return." God isn't saying, "Apologize to me and I might let you live." He's saying, "Turn toward me in order to find light and life once more."

## 351 | Believing without Seeing

> Then Jesus told him, "Because you have
> seen me, you have believed; blessed are those who
> have not seen and yet have believed."
>
> **— JOHN 20:29**

Many men don't appreciate the toxic patriarchal forces that women face every day, until they have daughters themselves. The loving proximity of fatherhood helps us see the lived reality of our children. This is a good thing. But like Thomas, who needed to see Jesus's wounds himself before he would believe, there is a higher way: believing without seeing. Jesus implies that believing people, even when you don't understand their experiences yourself, is more blessed.

## 352 | Becoming Memorable

> We remember before our God and Father your work
> produced by faith, your labor prompted by love, and your
> endurance inspired by hope in our Lord Jesus Christ.
>
> **— 1 THESSALONIANS 1:3**

Sometimes the simplest way to understand scripture is to turn the sentences around and read them backward. Flipping this verse gives a very clear picture: Hope in the Lord Jesus inspires endurance, love prompts labor, faith produces work, and all of this will make us memorable to others, who will pray for us. That's a pretty good summary of the way of Jesus. What are you most memorable for?

# 353 | How to Be Content

> *I know what it is to be in need, and I know what it is to have plenty. I have learned the secret of being content in any and every situation, whether well fed or hungry, whether living in plenty or in want. I can do all this through him who gives me strength.*
>
> **— PHILIPPIANS 4:12–13**

Reading one of the most popular Bible verses in context gives us a grittier picture than "Christian" coffee mugs usually portray. What exactly is it that Paul can do through Jesus? He can go hungry and live in want while remaining thankful. He can have plenty without becoming conceited or selfish. He can have strength for being content, something I pray we all find.

# 354 | Overflowing with Hope

> *May the God of hope fill you with all joy and peace as you trust in him, so that you may overflow with hope by the power of the Holy Spirit.*
>
> **— ROMANS 15:13**

In these days filled with fear and disagreement, when our churches and nations seem as divided as they've ever been, I think we need daily doses of hope. Thankfully, hope is one of the most persistent themes in scripture. As we come into these last few days of our year together, I pray that God fills you with hope this day and every day. May the Holy Spirit so fill you with hope, joy, and peace that you overflow.

# 355 | Radical Oneness

*My prayer is not for them alone. I pray also for those
who will believe in me through their message,
that all of them may be one, Father, just as you are in
me and I am in you. May they also be in us so
that the world may believe that you have sent me.*

**— JOHN 17:20-21**

The Father, Son, and Holy Spirit make up one mysterious
being in a union of love that cannot be defined or divided
and that has no equal. Remarkably, Jesus asks his Father
that everyone who follows him will find their way into oneness as well, oneness with each other and oneness with
God himself. This is a generous desire that really takes my
breath away. It also sobers me, because Jesus indicates
that the world's acceptance that he is the Son of God is
contingent on our unity with God and one another. That God
would entrust such high stakes to us is astonishing.

## Live Out the Word

Whom do you trust with your highest-stakes scenarios and
most precious possessions? How did they earn this trust?

Do you trust yourself in the same way? Does God
trust you?

What do you think the world would look like if we each
trusted one another this way? Thinking of your closest five
or ten friends, what could you practically do toward this?

Join your prayers with Jesus and ask God to draw you
into oneness with your fellow brothers and sisters and
with him.

# 356 | He Chose a Donkey

> *Rejoice greatly, Daughter Zion! Shout, Daughter Jerusalem! See, your king comes to you, righteous and victorious, lowly and riding on a donkey, on a colt, the foal of a donkey.*
>
> **— ZECHARIAH 9:9**

Rejoice, the prophet writes, for salvation and righteousness are coming at last. Evil will be defeated. Injustice thwarted. Oppressors overthrown. Captives freed. The king is coming and all shall be made right. The Lord of all creation rides upon . . . a donkey. Uncomfortable, ungainly, and unglamorous. A lowly and humble beast carries our anointed savior inexorably toward us.

# 357 | The New Order

> *"Look! God's dwelling place is now among the people, and he will dwell with them. They will be his people, and God himself will be with them and be their God. 'He will wipe every tear from their eyes. There will be no more death' or mourning or crying or pain, for the old order of things has passed away."*
>
> **— REVELATION 21:3-4**

The old order of death and sadness and pain is not forever. We who have been transformed by Jesus carry the new order within us, where radical acceptance conquers strongest fear, outrageous compassion heals deepest wounds, and the light of love casts out all shadows. This is the future God is gently and graciously guiding all things toward.

# 358 | How Vast This Love

> *I pray that you, being rooted and established
> in love, may have power, together with all the
> Lord's holy people, to grasp how wide
> and long and high and deep is the love of Christ.*
>
> **— EPHESIANS 3:17B–18**

Ephesians, the most universally applicable of all the church letters attributed to Paul, is an exhortation toward unity and holiness in the collected body of Jesus followers. And what is necessary for such unity? That we might somehow comprehend and grab hold of how inclusive and expansive God's love really is. How vast is this love?

# 359 | The Lion and the Lamb

> *After this I looked, and there before me was a great
> multitude that no one could count, from every nation,
> tribe, people and language, standing before the throne
> and before the Lamb. They were wearing white robes
> and were holding palm branches in their hands.*
>
> **— REVELATION 7:9**

In John's revelation, the Messiah who conquers death and defeats sin sounds like a roaring lion but is revealed as a slain lamb. Jesus's humble way of others-centered, co-suffering love will eventually melt even the hardest of hearts. A multitude that no one can count, billions from every race and people of this earth, will one day stand side-by-side, worshipping and praising the Lamb, who is God.

# 360 | The Return of the King

> *The LORD will be king over the whole earth. On that day*
> *there will be one LORD, and his name the only name.*
>
> **— ZECHARIAH 14:9**

This same Jesus who walked the dusty streets of Jerusalem, opened blind eyes, and raised small girls from the dead—and who lives in you—also happens to be king over all creation. One day, this humble servant whose warhorse is a donkey will be seen by all for who he really is, and every knee will bow, and every tongue confess that Jesus is God and God alone is Lord of the cosmos. And the King will be pleased to bring justice and peace to all.

# 361 | To Gaze Is to Dwell

> *One thing I ask from the LORD, this only do I seek:*
> *that I may dwell in the house of the LORD*
> *all the days of my life, to gaze on the beauty of the*
> *LORD and to seek him in his temple.*
>
> **— PSALM 27:4**

Until that final day when God transforms the cosmos and brings forth new heavens and a new earth, we live in the tension of desire. Through contemplation, we can channel that tension and gaze on Jesus within us, capturing a fresh vision of his love every day. If you spend enough time in silent prayer and adoration, you will discover a beautiful thing: You already live in the house of the Lord.

## 362 | Immeasurably More

*Now to him who is able to do immeasurably more
than all we ask or imagine, according
to his power that is at work within us, to him be
glory in the church and in Christ Jesus
throughout all generations, for ever and ever! Amen.*

**— EPHESIANS 3:20-21**

I hope that you've learned more about God during this journey together. I hope you've been challenged to trust Jesus more and even encounter his Spirit in new ways. No matter how far we come in our walk with God, however, he will always surprise us and exceed our expectations. His power and love are so much more than we could ever imagine. Give him thanks for that.

## 363 | Onward!

*To him who is able to keep you from stumbling and to
present you before his glorious presence without fault
and with great joy—to the only God our Savior be glory,
majesty, power and authority, through Jesus Christ
our Lord, before all ages, now and forevermore! Amen.*

**— JUDE 1:24-25**

God's work is robust. Although his touch is delicate, he is not fragile, easily bruised, or quickly offended. You are going to trip up sometimes; you are going to lose track of his voice; you may even wonder if he is still with you. But he is. You are kept eternally in the hand of God, who draws you onward toward himself.

# 364 | Until Completion

*Being confident... that he who began a
good work in you will carry it on to
completion until the day of Christ Jesus.*

**— PHILIPPIANS 1:6**

As you journey onward, following Jesus through the guidance of the Holy Spirit, you're going to go places I couldn't imagine. That's the whole point. Following the Spirit will lead you into the best, most fulfilling kind of life. It won't always make sense, it won't always be easy, and it won't always please other people, but it will bring you to completion in him. This is your journey with God. Listen to the Spirit, find community, study the scriptures together, and learn to love one another. This is life.

# 365 | The Afterglow

*The grace of the Lord Jesus be with God's people. Amen.*

**— REVELATION 22:21**

Brother, thank you for journeying with me through scripture. It's been an honor. I join my prayer with that of John the Beloved Disciple and ask that all the grace of our Lord Jesus be with you. May peace and hope bubble up within you, and may you find the strength and wisdom to be a man of courage, compassion, and curiosity. May Jesus guide you onward. May his life burst forth within you and give you peace. May you feel the afterglow of your faithful ancestors, who would be so proud of the man you're becoming. Amen.

# Index

confession to a trusted
brother, 42
contemplation upon trust,
95, 183
dishonesty as compromising
trust, 118
divine life, trust as the
currency of, 104
fear, replacing with trust, 14
God as trustworthy, 19,
139, 182
grace and trust, moving
into, 49
in the guidance of the
Lord, 146
in the Holy Spirit, 35, 77, 109
intentional posture of trust,
111, 116
Jesus, trust in, 47, 55, 187
lessons of trust, 58, 158
trust in God, 16, 27, 33, 46,
47, 54, 63, 93, 100

# V

Value, 68, 99, 128
in embodied community
life, 50
meekness as a value, 69
mercy as a value, 70

pearl of great value, 35
sexual pleasure, God as
valuing, 107
toxic leadership, devaluing
actions of, 105
worthiness in the body of
Christ, 125

# W

Wisdom, 12, 15, 17, 103, 105, 188
community wisdom and
care, 23
elders, appreciating the
wisdom of, 117
the faithful and wise
servant, 77
as a gift of the Spirit, 157
maturity and the wise
man, 143
never too wise to learn, 112
Worship, 88
David, worship style of, 171
God as worthy of, 40, 45, 178
living sacrifice as proper
worship, 120
sacred worship, all work
as, 13
sacrificial worship under
the law, 49

## Acknowledgments

Many thanks to my editorial team for encouraging me to study and write about scripture in a way I hadn't planned on. Thank you to Jonathan Boerger and Ahmeda Mansaray-Richardson for linguistic and theological input. Many thanks to the Clarkes and Schelskes for housing and feeding me. To the countless pastors, scholars, and theologians who have formed me, including John and Carol Arnott, Greg Boyd, Brad Jersak, Wm. Paul Young, Cherith Nordling, Julie Canlis, Fr. John Behr, N.T. Wright, David Bentley Hart, Wendy Farley, Wayne Jacobsen, and so many others, thank you! To my guides in body, trauma, and healing, such as Aundi Kolber, Dr. Dan Siegel, Hillary McBride, Fr. Andrew Miller, Richard Schwartz, Henri Nouwen, and Thomas Merton, thank you for your courage. Maria Bergner, thank you for challenging me to get back into the Bible.

## About the Author

**Jonathan Puddle** is a contemplative, Jesus-following mystic, who helps people find God at work in their inner lives. His other books include the award-winning *You Are Enough: Learning to Love Yourself the Way God Loves You*. Having traveled the world and lived in many nations, he writes from a culturally rich and spiritually inclusive framework. Before becoming a writer, Jonathan spent ten years in charity leadership and he remains a visionary thinker with a strategic mind. A husband, father, and foster parent, Jonathan resides with his family in Guelph, Canada, where they pastor families and children at a local community church. Find his podcast and more at jonathanpuddle.com.